TRUST, THE PROCESS

A GUIDE TO USING TRUSTS AS A TOOL TO PROTECT & BUILD WEALTH IN MINORITY COMMUNITIES

Copyright © 2025 by Shannon R. Wright

All rights reserved. No part of this book may be reproduced, distributed, or transmitted in any form or by any means, including photocopying, recording, or other electronic or mechanical methods, without the prior written permission of the author, except in the case of brief quotations embodied in critical reviews and certain other noncommercial uses permitted by copyright law.

DISCLAIMER

The information provided in this book is intended for educational and informational purposes only and should not be construed as legal, tax, or financial advice. No attorney-client relationship is created by reading this book between the reader and the author, Shannon R. Wright, or The Law Office of Shannon R. Wright PLLC. Readers are advised that laws and regulations can vary widely by jurisdiction, and the content herein may not reflect the most up-to-date legal or regulatory developments. It is crucial for readers to consult a licensed attorney in their respective state or a qualified financial professional to address specific legal, financial, or estate planning needs.

The book strives to discuss cultural, historical, and financial issues with sensitivity and respect for diversity. Nonetheless, the author and publisher make no representations or warranties regarding the accuracy or completeness of the information provided. Readers are encouraged to approach the material critically, considering their individual circumstances and the broader societal context. The author and publisher disclaim any liability arising from reliance on the information contained within this book, and recommend seeking personalized advice from certified professionals.

ISBN: 979-8-9929743-0-0

Published by: Secure The Promise Publishing

Contact Information:
1914 J. N. Pease Place
Charlotte, NC 28262
704-738-3837
info@srwrightlaw.com
www.securethepromise.org

First Edition: March 2025

Contents

Chapter 1
The Historical Landscape of Wealth in African American
Communities   8

Chapter 2
Trusts Explained - A Vehicle for Generational Wealth   16

Chapter 3
Crafting Your Trust - A Comprehensive Approach   26

Chapter 4
Funding the Trust: Asset Allocation Strategies   42

Chapter 5
Trust and Taxation: A Comprehensive Guide
to the Implications for Revocable Trusts   48

Chapter 6
Comprehensive Tax Strategies for Trusts   56

Chapter 7
Estate Planning as a Family Conversation—
Understanding the Roles of Trustees and Beneficiaries   68

Chapter 8
From Vision to Reality: Effective Strategies for
Managing Revocable Trusts   78

Chapter 9
The Art of Legacy Letters - A Canvas for Life's
Wisdom and Treasures Beyond Wealth   88

Chapter 10
Overcoming Barriers to Estate Planning   98

Trust, the Process

The Guide to Using Trusts to Build and Protect Generational Wealth in the African American Community

Preface: Inspired by True Events

⊃ Reels Family Story

I first came upon the story of the Reels family while watching the 2023 documentary **Silver Dollar Road**. As I sat there, captivated by their decades-long battle to hold onto their sixty five acre coastal property in North Carolina, I couldn't help but feel a deep connection to their struggle. Their story, which unfolded for more than over forty years, is one of courage, resilience, and heartbreak—a family fighting to preserve what their great-grandfather Elijah Reels had painstakingly acquired in 1911, just one generation after slavery.

The Reels family's fight reminded me of the close-knit community where I grew up, a place where land and property were more than just assets; they were the bedrock of our identity, the embodiment of our history, and a promise to future generations. Watching their struggle, I felt compelled to do more. It became clear to me their story is not just a singular tale of injustice but a reflection of a broader issue that has plagued African American families for generations.

This story stirred something deep within me, urging me to speak out and take action. The parallels between their experience and the experiences of countless other African American families who have seen their wealth eroded or outright stolen due to systemic racism are undeniable. The Reels family's plight is a stark reminder of how easily generational wealth can be lost when it is not protected by proper legal measures, such as trusts.

As we explore the history of wealth in African American communities, the Reels family's story serves as a powerful illustration of why estate planning is so critical. It is not just about accumulating wealth; it is about protecting it, preserving it, and ensuring it can be passed down through generations. This story has reinforced my belief we must do more to safeguard our legacies, and it has inspired me to share the tools and knowledge needed to protect our hard-earned gains. The Reels family's struggle is a call to action, reminding us all of the importance of taking control of our financial futures, so our children and grandchildren can inherit more than just memories—they can inherit a secure future.

The resilience of the Reels family not only touched my heart but also ignited a passion to empower others with the knowledge to protect their legacies.

Introduction:
ROOTS AND REFLECTIONS

As a child, I was always eager to listen to adults discussing community news and daily concerns. This curiosity undoubtedly fueled my interest in our family history and my own past. Growing up in the low country of South Carolina, I relished the abundant stories from our community's past, including stories of my grandparents and of the old days.

I was born in a small town that formed around sawmills and textile plants. Desegregation came to my town the same year I was born. It was also the year the last class graduated from the black high school, Rosemary. Most of the families either had a parent who worked in the steel mill, paper mill, knitting mill, or pulpwood trucking. It was a tight-knit Southern town where parents "got off" from work around four or five in the afternoon. Dinner was at six, and Walter Cronkite came on at 7:30 p.m. There were prayer meetings on Tuesday and Bible class was on Wednesday evening. Up Jump the Devil, the little hole in the wall on Jones Ave, would get the party started about 9:30 p.m. on Fridays. There was a pool table in the middle of the floor, juke box, and pickled pig feet in the jar on the counter. Life was slow, somewhat simple, and warm like I imagined a cocoon would be. Home, the place from which I came. My little town had a large African American population, and today it's predominantly African American. It's not the same cute little town it once was it's now fighting to survive. The past few decades haven't been easy due to economic shifts and our economy moving away from manufacturing over the past forty years.

My parents are baby boomers. I am a part of the generation that came along after the unrest of the 60s and civil rights struggles filled with protests and marches. They lived their first twenty years mainly under the oppression of the Jim Crow era and witnessed significant changes. They saw the type of change that allowed them to talk about the harshness of the old days and how my siblings, friends, and I were blessed to not have the experience of such in-your-face oppression. My grandparents' and parents' generations were hardworking and made sacrifices so their grandchildren and children would not have to travel such a difficult road. Almost sixty years after the Civil Rights Act of 1964 and the Voting Rights Act of 1965, a lot has changed but not nearly as much as we had hoped. Economically, African Americans still face huge wealth inequality, and sometimes the racial wealth gap seems to be insurmountable.

I'm so thankful for the security and warmth my childhood brought, but that time is long gone. I've learned more about the harshness of this world and what it means for my people. I am not here to offer a manifesto or a miraculous solution, but rather to share a practical tool that could safeguard the gains of our community. What I am here to do is open the door to one of the tools we should be using to protect the things we have gained and offer some proper ways to pass those resources on to our children and our children's children. My journey has brought me to the practice of law and the not-so-sexy but very much needed area of law called estate planning. Specifically, I've found myself fascinated with trusts and how these powerful instruments work.

This book is an invitation to explore the use of trusts as a vehicle for building and protecting generational wealth. It is a guide meant to explain the complexities of legal and financial planning and to provide a roadmap for those who seek to ensure their legacies endure. Through the chapters that follow, we will explore the rich history, the current landscape, and the potential future of African American economic empowerment, all through the lens of trust-based estate planning.

Join me on this journey of discovery and empowerment.

Chapter 1

The Historical Landscape of Wealth in African American Communities

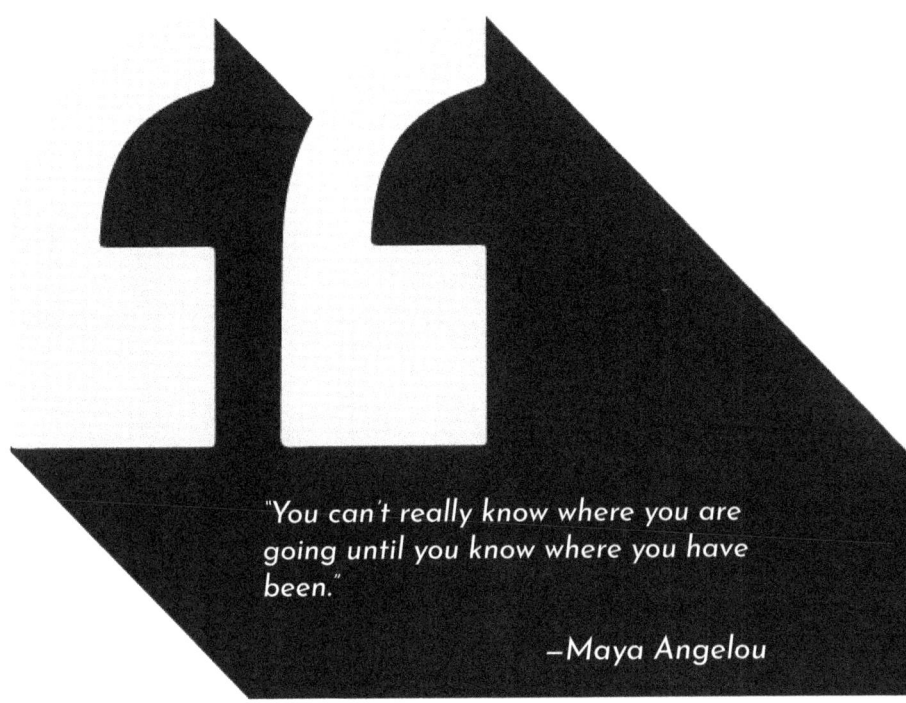

"You can't really know where you are going until you know where you have been."

—Maya Angelou

Throughout the sprawling landscapes of America, from the bustling cities to the quiet rural areas, the story of African American wealth accumulation is a complex tapestry, woven with threads of historical adversity and resilience. This narrative isn't just about numbers; it's about the lived experiences of generations, the systemic barriers they've faced, and the unyielding spirit of a community seeking equitable economic opportunities.

The gap in wealth between African Americans and their white counterparts is stark and telling. As highlighted by recent Federal Reserve data, African Americans on average own significantly less wealth compared to their white counterparts, illustrating a persistent racial wealth gap. This statistic is a somber reminder of a history marred by exclusion and discrimination. It represents the cumulative effect of policies and practices that have systematically denied African Americans access to wealth-building opportunities.

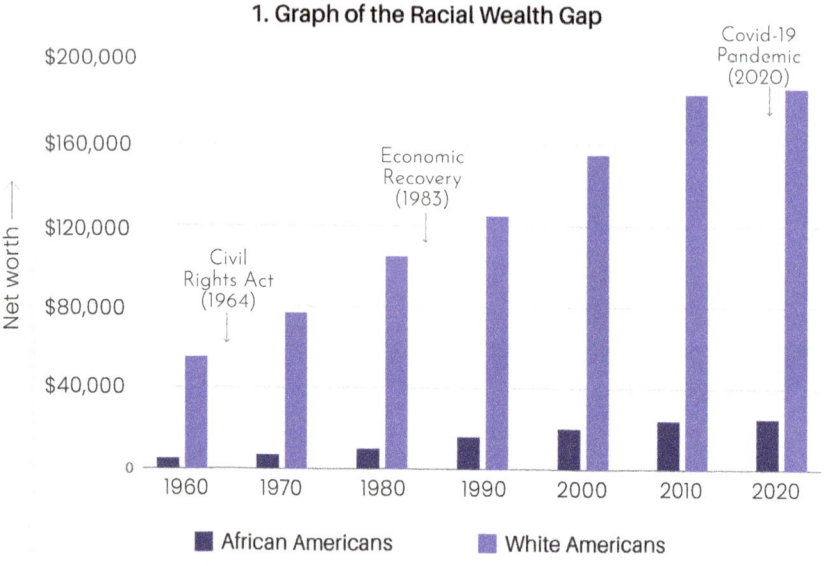

The legacy of the Great Recession further exacerbated this divide. Before the economic downturn in 2008, African American wealth was already substantially lower than that of white families, underscoring longstanding economic disparities.

This gap is more than just an economic issue; it's a reflection of deeper societal inequities. African Americans have historically faced greater challenges in accumulating personal savings, often grappling with negative income shocks and limited access to emergency funds. The result is a precarious financial situation where many are just one emergency away from financial instability.

The roots of this disparity run deep, tracing back to the very foundations of American history. From the era of slavery, through the Jim Crow laws, to modern practices like redlining and employment discrimination, African Americans have been systematically hindered in their pursuit of economic prosperity. The wealth gap is not just a symptom of economic inequality, but also of a broader societal issue that includes unequal access to education, healthcare, and housing.

A deeper examination of specific discriminatory laws and policies reveals the profound impact they had on the economic status of African American communities. For instance, the GI Bill, formally known as the Servicemen's Readjustment Act of 1944, is often celebrated for helping millions of returning World War II veterans gain access to higher education and homeownership. However, the implementation of the GI Bill was marred by widespread racial discrimination. African American veterans were systematically denied the same benefits their white counterparts received. Many were excluded from educational institutions due to segregation policies and were frequently steered away from using the mortgage and loan benefits to acquire property, leading to significant disparities in post-war economic opportunities.

Similarly, the Federal Housing Administration (FHA) mortgage practices played a pivotal role in shaping the housing landscape in the United States. Through redlining practices, the FHA explicitly refused to insure mortgages in and near African American neighborhoods — a policy that not only devalued properties in these areas but also locked out black families from accessing affordable home loans. This policy hindered their ability to build wealth through homeownership, one of the most crucial avenues for wealth accumulation in America.

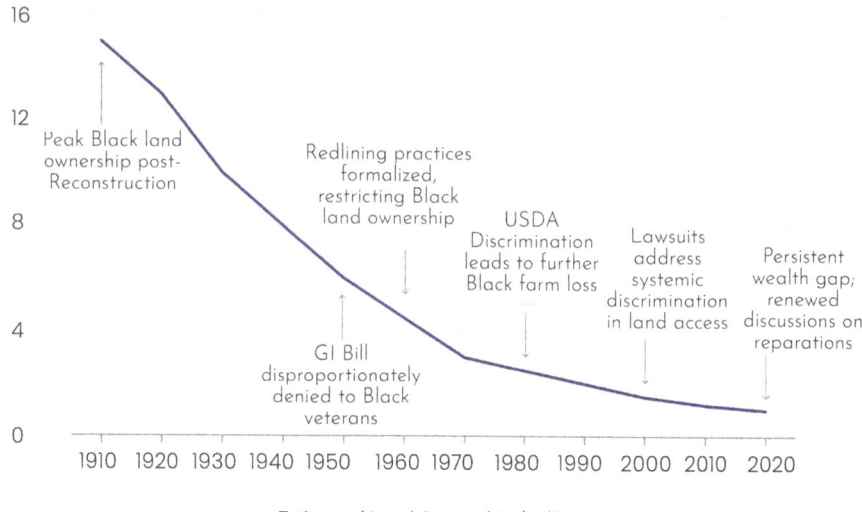

These examples illustrate not just isolated instances of discrimination, but a systemic pattern that hindered African Americans from building wealth across generations. Understanding these specific impacts provides a clearer picture of the economic challenges many African American families continue to face today, underscoring the need for targeted reforms that address these historical injustices.

Despite these challenges, the African American community has shown remarkable resilience and determination. The struggle for equality and justice, epitomized by the Civil Rights Movement, has led to significant progress in many areas. However, when it comes to economic equity, there is still a long road ahead.

The disparities extend beyond simple metrics of wealth and income. Homeownership rates, business ownership, and access to retirement savings are all areas where African Americans lag behind their white counterparts. When we do own assets, they are often of lesser value due to systemic factors like market discrimination and segregation.

The conversation about wealth in African American communities cannot be completed without acknowledging the role of debt. African American households often incur higher-cost debts, frequently characterized by higher interest rates and less favorable terms. This not only limits their ability to accumulate wealth but also makes them more vulnerable to economic downturns.

Looking ahead, targeted policy interventions are necessary to bridge this wealth gap. The concept of targeted universalism offers a promising approach, recognizing that while the goal of economic prosperity is universal, the paths to achieving it are varied and must be tailored to address the specific challenges faced by African Americans.

3. Timeline of Key Events Affecting Wealth

1930
New Deal Programs Exclude Black Workers

1934-1968
Redlining and Housing Discrimination

1944
GI Bill Benefits Denied to Black veterans

1964-1968
Civil Rights & Fair Housing Acts Passed

1980s-1990s
War on Drugs & Mass Incarceration

2008
Great Recession & Subprime Mortgage Crisis

2020
COVID-19 Pandemic & Racial Wealth Gap Awareness

As we turn the pages of history, we are reminded the story of African American wealth is not just a tale of struggle, but also one of strength, perseverance, and hope. It is a narrative that underscores the need for continued advocacy, policy reform, and community empowerment. In the quest for economic equality, the African American community stands resilient, ready to shape a more equitable and prosperous future.

The Importance of Rebuilding Trust in Legal and Financial Institutions

In the rich and complex history of African American communities, the journey towards economic empowerment has often been hindered by a deep-seated mistrust of legal and financial systems. This mistrust, born from a legacy of systemic injustices, has had a profound impact on estate planning within the community. As Reetu Pepoff eloquently states in "The Intersection of Racial Inequities and Estate Planning" in the ACTEC Law Journal, "Many African Americans may intentionally choose to rely on the laws of intestacy based on the notion that the land will remain in the family indefinitely because it will be passed on to the decedent's heirs. It is rooted in the belief that living on the property and paying the real estate taxes and expenses solidifies the ownership of the property."

This perspective, while understandable, overlooks the complexities and potential pitfalls of intestate succession, particularly in the context of African American wealth preservation. The cases of James Brown, Aretha Franklin, Chadwick Boseman, and Prince, who all passed away without clear estate plans, starkly illustrate the challenges and disputes that can arise in the absence of deliberate estate planning.

The reluctance to engage with estate planning reflects a broader narrative of distrust towards "the system." This sentiment is not baseless; it stems from a history of African Americans being denied fair access to legal and financial resources. However, this avoidance can lead to unintended consequences, especially when properties are passed down as tenancies-in-common under intestacy laws, which govern the distribution of a person's estate when they die without a valid will. This type of ownership can make properties vulnerable to forced partition sales, a common occurrence in Black and Indigenous People of Color (BIPOC) communities, often resulting in families losing ancestral lands when they are forced to sell and then they are compensated for less than their worth.

This issue transcends African American communities, as evidenced by land losses experienced by Hispanics in New Mexico and Native Hawaiians, also due to partition sales. These shared experiences across different communities highlight the universal importance of informed estate planning.

To address this, there is a need for concerted efforts to educate and empower African American communities about the benefits of estate planning. This includes making legal advice accessible and reframing estate planning as a tool for empowerment and protection. By doing so, estate planning can be seen not just as a legal formality, but as a critical step in safeguarding generational wealth and ensuring its rightful transfer.

The path forward involves rebuilding trust in the legal and financial systems. This requires a shift in how these systems interact with African American communities, demonstrating a commitment to fairness and equity. Estate planning, in this light, becomes a powerful instrument for securing legacies and fostering generational prosperity.

As we reflect on this chapter of our history, we recognize the journey towards economic equality is not just about accumulating wealth; it's about building trust and using legal tools as a means of empowerment. The goal is to ensure the hard-earned gains of generations are preserved and passed on, solidifying the foundations for a prosperous future.

Chapter 2

Trusts Explained - A Vehicle for Generational Wealth

> *"Generational wealth isn't just built with money—it's built with knowledge, foresight, and the will to protect what matters most."*

In my practice, I often meet individuals who know they need to do something about their estate planning but don't know where to start. One of the first steps is understanding the difference between a will and a trust—and more importantly, how a trust can help avoid probate, making assets available to loved ones in a seamless or near-seamless way.

Trust saves time, money, and stress while also providing control and privacy over how assets are distributed. In this chapter, we'll explore the different types of trusts, breaking down the pros and cons of each. Because no two families are alike, the right trust depends on factors such as family structure, financial situation, age, number of beneficiaries, and their needs. By the end of this chapter, you'll have a clearer understanding of which trust might work best for you and your loved ones.

With a clear understanding of the historical challenges to wealth in African American communities, the necessity of trusts becomes undeniable. Trusts are more than legal documents; they are instruments of empowerment, breaking cycles of financial instability and securing economic independence for future generations.

Each type of trust serves a distinct purpose:

- **Revocable Trusts:**
  Allow modifications during the settlor's lifetime and help avoid probate.

- **Irrevocable Trusts:**
  Provide protection from creditors and potential estate tax benefits.

- **Living Trusts:**
  Manage assets during the settlor's lifetime, ensuring continuity.

- **Testamentary Trusts:**
  Activated after death, structuring wealth distribution through a will.

4. Pie Chart of Trust Types

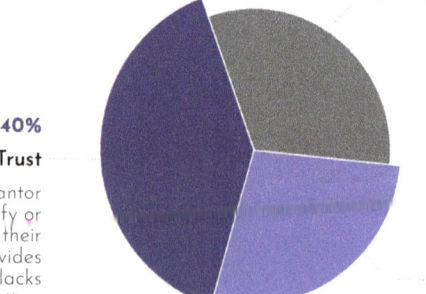

32%
Testamentary Trust
Established through a will and takes effect after the grantor's death. Used for estate planning and beneficiary control.

40%
Revocable Trust
Allows the grantor to modify or revoke during their lifetime. Provides flexibility but lacks asset protection.

28%
Irrevocable Trust
Cannot be changes once established. Offers tax benefits and asset protection..

Debunking the Trust Myth

NOT JUST FOR THE WEALTHY

A common misconception is that trusts are exclusive to the wealthy. In reality, trusts are invaluable tools for anyone looking to protect assets, minimize legal disputes, and ensure financial stability for their loved ones. Even modest estates can benefit from trusts, particularly in avoiding probate, ensuring privacy, and protecting assets from mismanagement.

Trusts are more than financial tools—they are commitments to the future. Whether it's a family home, savings, or personal treasures, placing assets in a trust secures them for future generations. By exploring the types of trusts in detail, you'll understand how they serve as proactive estate planning strategies tailored to individual needs.

Key Roles in a Trust

At the heart of every trust are three key roles:

- *Settlor (Grantor)*
  The person who establishes the trust and transfers assets into it.

- *Trustee*
  The individual or institution responsible for managing the trust.

- *Beneficiary*
  The person(s) who will receive the trust's assets as designated.

A well-structured trust allows the settlor to control the flow of wealth, ensuring assets are used responsibly while shielding them from risks like legal claims and unnecessary taxation.

Revocable Living Trusts
FLEXIBILITY & CONTROL

A revocable living trust is one of the most popular estate planning tools because it provides flexibility, privacy, and probate avoidance while allowing the settlor to retain control over assets.

Advantages of a Revocable Trust

- **Avoids Probate:**
  Assets bypass the court system, ensuring a quicker and private transfer.

- **Maintains Privacy:**
  Unlike wills, which become public record, trusts remain confidential.

- **Flexible & Adjustable:**
  The settlor can modify or revoke the trust at any time.

- **Protects Beneficiaries:**
  Allows structured inheritance distribution, reducing risks of financial mismanagement.

Limitations to Consider

- **Not a Shield from Creditors:**
  Since the settlor retains control, creditors may still access assets.

- **Requires Proper Funding:**
  If assets are not transferred into the trust, probate may still be necessary.

- **No Immediate Tax Benefits:**
  Unlike irrevocable trusts, revocable trusts do not reduce estate taxes during the settlor's lifetime.

Revocable Trust in Action

Consider an elderly homeowner who places their property in a revocable trust. If they become incapacitated, their designated trustee can manage the property seamlessly, avoiding the need for a court-appointed guardian. Upon death, the property transfers directly to their heirs without probate delays.

Irrevocable Trusts:
LONG-TERM WEALTH PROTECTION

In contrast to revocable trusts, an irrevocable trust cannot be modified after creation, offering stronger legal and financial protections.

Key Benefits of Irrevocable Trusts

- **Protects Assets from Creditors & Lawsuits:**
  Assets placed in the trust no longer belong to the settlor, shielding them from legal claims.

- **Potential Tax Advantages:**
  Reduces taxable estate value, minimizing estate taxes for high-net-worth individuals.

- **Preserves Government Benefits:**
  Beneficiaries with special needs can receive inheritances without losing eligibility for programs like Medicaid.

- **Ensures Legacy Protection:**
  Settlor can dictate precise terms for distribution, preventing wasteful spending.

Challenges of an Irrevocable Trust

- **Loss of Control:**
  Once assets are transferred, the settlor cannot reclaim them.

- **Complex Setup:**
  Establishing and managing an irrevocable trust requires strategic planning and legal guidance.

- **Potential Taxation on Trust Income:**
  The trust itself may be taxed at a higher rate depending on its structure.

> **EXAMPLE**
> **WEALTH PRESERVATION**

A business owner places assets in an irrevocable trust to protect them from creditors in case of future lawsuits. This proactive move ensures that even in times of financial distress, their family's wealth remains secure and untouchable.

Testamentary Trusts:
STRUCTURED INHERITANCE

A **testamentary trust** is created through a will and only takes effect **after the settlor's death**. These trusts provide structured inheritance distribution, making them ideal for **young beneficiaries or complex family situations**.

Advantages of Testamentary Trusts

- **Controlled Distribution:**
  Prevents lump-sum inheritances, ensuring responsible financial management.

- **Protection for Minors & Dependents:**
  Parents can designate funds for their children's education, housing, or milestones.

- **Customizable Terms:**
  Allows the settlor to define specific conditions for asset distribution.

Limitations of Testamentary Trusts

- **Subject to Probate:**
  Since it is tied to a will, it does not bypass probate.

- **Delayed Activation:**
  Only becomes operational after the settlor's death, requiring patience from beneficiaries.

- **Less Privacy:**
  As part of probate proceedings, some details may become public.

EXAMPLE
PROTECTING A YOUNG HEIR

A single mother sets up a testamentary trust in her will, specifying that her children will receive portions of their inheritance at ages 18, 25, and 30, rather than in a single lump sum. This structured approach protects against financial mismanagement and ensures long-term security.

Making the Right Choice

Choosing the right type of trust depends on your financial goals, family situation, and level of control desired. Here's a quick comparison:

Trust Type	Best For	Flexibility	Probate Avoidance	Creditor Protection	Estate Tax Benefits
Revocable Trust	Avoiding probate, maintaining control	High	Yes	No	No
Irrevocable Trust	Asset protection, tax minimization	None	Yes	Yes	Yes
Testamentary Trust	Structuring inheritance for minors/dependents	Moderate	No	No	Some

By taking action today, you ensure your wealth is protected, managed, and passed down with intention, securing financial stability for generations to come.

As we transition from exploring the different types of trusts to the practical steps of trust establishment, it is essential to approach this process with clarity and intention. Establishing a trust is more than a legal transaction—it is an act of foresight and responsibility, a commitment to ensuring that your hard-earned wealth serves as a foundation for future generations.

In the next chapter, we will dive into the practical steps of creating a trust, guiding you through key decisions that shape this vital component of estate planning. From choosing the right type of trust to understanding the roles of trustees and beneficiaries, we will navigate the path to establishing a trust that aligns with your vision for a lasting legacy.

While the process may seem complex, it stands as a powerful testament to the resilience and dedication of those who seek to uplift and empower their families and communities through thoughtful, strategic estate planning.

5. Asset Protection Strategies Diagram

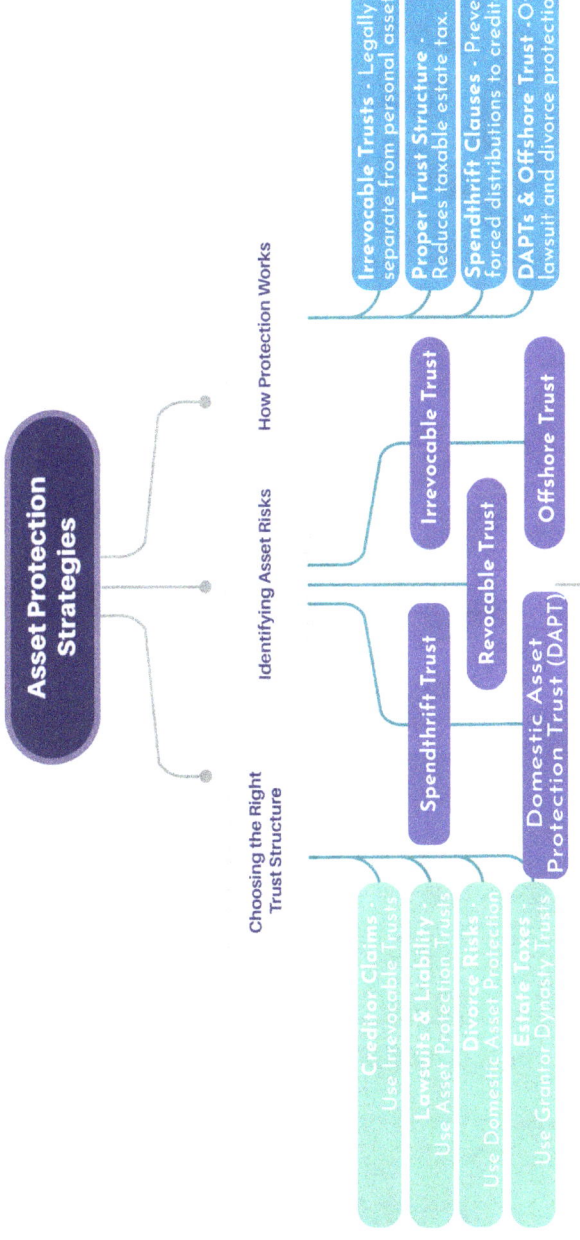

Chapter 3

Crafting Your Trust - A Comprehensive Approach

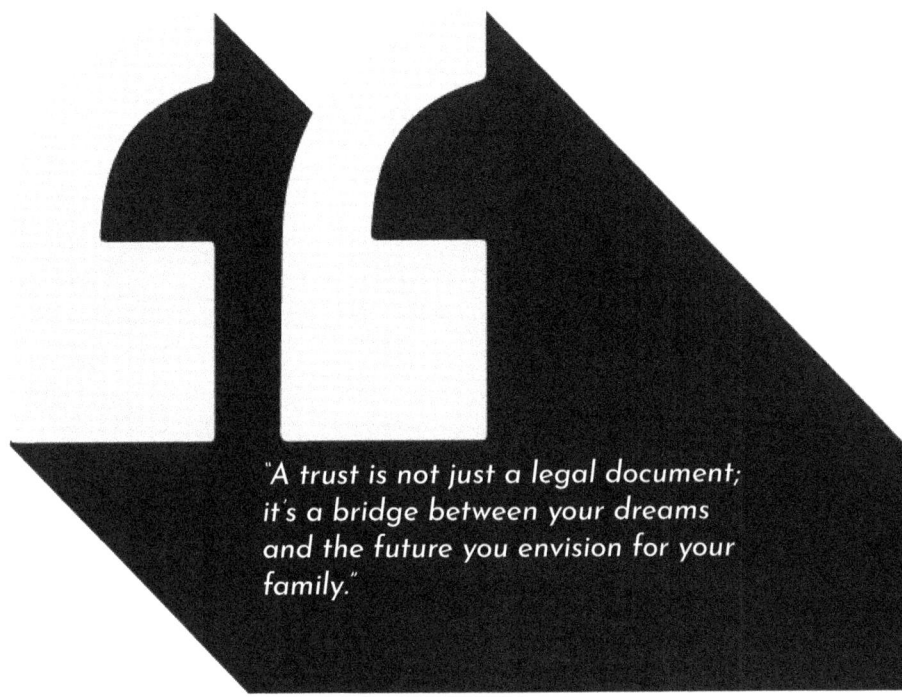

"A trust is not just a legal document; it's a bridge between your dreams and the future you envision for your family."

Deciding on the Type of Trust:

NAVIGATING YOUR OPTIONS

Selecting the right type of trust is a critical first step in trust creation, one that lays the foundation for how your assets will be managed and distributed. This decision is shaped by a multitude of factors, each reflecting your unique financial landscape and estate planning goals. Here is a quick overview of the types of trusts we have already covered.

Revocable Trusts: Flexibility and Adaptability

As previously discussed, for many, a revocable living trust is an appealing choice due to its flexibility. Revocable trusts are ideal for individuals who want control over their assets during their lifetime, offering the flexibility to modify the trust's terms in response to life changes like marriage, the birth or adoption of children, or significant financial shifts. A revocable trust allows you to adjust its provisions in response to life events such as marriage, the birth of children, acquisition or disposal of significant assets, or changes in financial goals.

Individual vs. Shared Trusts: Personal vs. Joint Asset Management:

When considering a revocable trust, you'll need to choose between an individual or a shared trust. An individual trust is ideal if you wish to manage your own separate property, while a shared trust, typically set up by spouses, is designed to manage jointly held assets. This choice hinges on the nature of your asset ownership—whether they are solely yours or co-owned with your spouse.

Irrevocable Trusts: Long-Term Security and Tax Benefits

Though less flexible, irrevocable trusts offer long-term security and can provide significant tax benefits. If you have substantial assets and are looking to minimize estate taxes or protect your assets from creditors and legal judgments, an irrevocable trust might be the right choice. Due to the permanent nature of irrevocable trusts, where terms cannot be altered once established, comprehensive planning and careful consideration are crucial prior to setting up this type of trust.

Testamentary Trusts: Structured Posthumous Asset Distribution

For those who prefer to focus on how their assets will be managed and distributed after their death, testamentary trusts present a viable option. Testamentary trusts, established within a will, only activate after the trustor's death, facilitating a predetermined method of estate distribution that adheres closely to the trustor's stipulated desires.

Factors Influencing Your Trust Choice

Several key considerations should guide your decision:

- **Asset Type and Value:**
  The nature and value of your assets play a crucial role. For instance, high-value or complex assets like business interests might benefit more from the protective structure of an irrevocable trust.

- **Privacy and Control Needs:**
  If maintaining privacy and control over your assets during your lifetime is a priority, a revocable trust is often more suitable.

- **Estate Tax Implications:**
  For estates that may face significant tax liabilities, an irrevocable trust can provide essential tax benefits.

- **Future Changes and Flexibility:**
  Consider how likely you are to need to make changes to your trust in the future. A revocable trust offers the adaptability to modify terms as your situation evolves.

- **Family Dynamics and Beneficiary Needs:**
  The nature of your family relationships and the specific needs of your beneficiaries can also influence the type of trust you choose. For example, if you have minor children or beneficiaries with special needs, specific types of trusts can provide for their unique requirements.

The choice of trust type is a deeply personal decision that sets the stage for how your estate will be managed and your legacy preserved. It requires a thoughtful balance between your current financial situation, future aspirations, and the well-being of your beneficiaries. Understanding the nuances of each trust type and aligning them with your individual needs and goals is paramount in this process. As you embark on this journey, remember that your trust is more than a legal document; it is a reflection of your life's work, values, and hopes for the future.

Choosing a Successor Trustee:

A DECISION OF TRUST AND RESPONSIBILITY

The role of a successor trustee in a trust is akin to a captain steering a ship—they are entrusted with the responsibility of navigating the trust through the complexities of asset management and distribution. Therefore, selecting the right person or entity for this role is a decision that requires careful consideration and foresight.

Understanding the Role of a Successor Trustee

- **Management and Distribution of Assets:**
  The successor trustee is responsible for managing the trust's assets according to the terms set out in the trust document. This includes making decisions about investment, distribution to beneficiaries, and handling any administrative tasks associated with the trust.

- **Acting in Times of Incapacity or Death:**
  In the event of your incapacity or death, the successor trustee steps in to manage the trust. This requires not only a deep understanding of your wishes and the trust's terms but also the ability to make prudent decisions under potentially challenging circumstances.

Qualities to Look for in a Successor Trustee

- **Trustworthiness:**
  Above all, the successor trustee must be someone you trust implicitly. They will have considerable control over your assets and the authority to make decisions that will impact your beneficiaries.

- **Objectivity and Impartiality:**
  It's crucial the trustee can act objectively and fairly, especially if there are multiple beneficiaries with differing interests. They must be able to navigate family dynamics and potential conflicts while adhering to the trust's terms.

- **Financial Acumen:**
  A good understanding of financial matters and investment strategies is beneficial, particularly for trusts with complex assets.

➲ **Organizational Skills:**
Managing a trust requires organizational skills, from keeping detailed records to staying on top of legal and tax obligations.

Options for Successor Trustees

➲ **Family Members or Friends:**
Choosing a family member or a close friend as a trustee is common but consider the dynamics this might create among beneficiaries and the individual's capability to manage the trust effectively.

➲ **Professional Trustees:**
A bank or trust company can serve as a professional trustee, offering expertise, experience, and neutrality. This option can be particularly advantageous for complex trusts or situations where family dynamics may complicate trust administration.

➲ **Co-Trustees:**
Appointing co-trustees, either individuals or a combination of an individual and a professional, can balance personal knowledge of your wishes with professional expertise in trust management.

Communicating with Your Chosen Trustee

Once you have selected a successor trustee, it is crucial to communicate your decision and discuss the responsibilities and expectations associated with the role. Provide them with a copy of the trust document and any other relevant information to ensure they understand the scope of their duties.

The Cornerstone of Effective Trust Management

Choosing a successor trustee is a decision that anchors the effective management and execution of your trust. It's a role that demands integrity, competence, and a commitment to upholding your estate planning objectives. This choice not only impacts the administration of your trust but also the legacy you leave behind, making it one of the most significant decisions in the trust creation process. By selecting the right successor trustee, you ensure your trust is in capable hands, ready to honor your wishes and protect the interests of your beneficiaries.

Identifying Beneficiaries and Setting Trust Rules:
A DELIBERATE PROCESS

When establishing a trust, the selection of beneficiaries and the establishment of trust rules are among the most personal and impactful decisions you will make. This step is where the intent of your trust takes shape, turning your financial legacy into a meaningful and lasting impact.

Selecting Beneficiaries

- *Family and Spouses:*
  The most common beneficiaries are family members, including spouses, children, and grandchildren. Consider the individual needs and circumstances of each potential beneficiary, such as their age, financial literacy, and personal goals.

- **Extended Family and Friends:**
  You may also choose to include extended family members or close friends as beneficiaries, particularly if they have been integral to your life or you wish to provide for their future.

- **Charities and Foundations:**
  For those who are philanthropically inclined, including charities or foundations as beneficiaries can be a way to extend your legacy beyond your immediate circle and make a lasting impact on causes you care about.

- **Trusts for Minors:**
  If your beneficiaries are minors, setting up a trust for their benefit can ensure they are provided for until they reach a responsible age. This can include stipulations for education, living expenses, and other support.

Setting Trust Rules

- **Distribution Guidelines:**
  Clearly outline how and when beneficiaries will receive assets. You might specify age milestones, educational achievements, or other life events as triggers for distribution.

- **Conditions for Distribution:**
  You can set conditions that beneficiaries must meet to receive their inheritance, such as completing a degree, entering a specific profession, or reaching certain personal milestones.

- **Protective Measures:**
  Consider provisions to protect the trust's assets from potential issues like beneficiaries' creditors, divorce settlements, or imprudent financial decisions.

- **Special Needs Considerations:**
  If any beneficiaries have special needs, tailor the trust to provide for their care and lifestyle without compromising their eligibility for government assistance.

- **Charitable Giving:**
  If including charitable giving, specify the amounts, timing, and conditions under which the distributions will be made to ensure your philanthropic goals are met.

The Importance of Clarity and Flexibility

The rules you set for your trust should be clear to avoid ambiguity and potential disputes. However, consider including some degree of flexibility to account for unforeseen changes in beneficiaries' circumstances or needs. This balance between clarity and adaptability is crucial in ensuring your trust effectively reflects your intentions and adapts to future challenges and opportunities.

Tailoring Your Trust to Reflect Your Values

Identifying beneficiaries and setting the rules of your trust is a process that requires deep reflection on your values, goals, and the legacy you wish to leave. This step is not just about asset distribution; it's about shaping the future impact of your wealth and the message it conveys to your beneficiaries. In crafting these aspects of your trust, you are not only defining who will benefit from your life's work but also how those benefits will be realized and the values they will promote.

Collaborating with an Attorney to Draft Your Trust Document:

THE LEGAL FOUNDATION

The creation of your trust document is a pivotal step in establishing your trust, one that lays the legal foundation for how your assets will be managed and distributed. This is a task best undertaken with the guidance and expertise of an experienced estate planning attorney.

The Role of an Attorney in Drafting Your Trust

- **Expert Guidance:**
  An attorney specializing in estate planning can provide invaluable advice on the nuances of trust law, helping to ensure your trust aligns with legal requirements and your personal goals.

- **Customization of Terms:**
  Every trust is unique. An attorney can help tailor the terms of your trust to your specific situation, ensuring your assets are distributed according to your wishes and your beneficiaries are adequately provided for.

- **Addressing Complex Issues:**
  If your estate includes complex assets, such as businesses or investments, or if you have a blended family or other unique circumstances, an attorney can help navigate these complexities to specify your wishes within your trust document.

Additional Legal Considerations

⊃ **Power of Attorney for Assets Outside the Trust:**
Not all assets may be included in your trust. For such assets, consider establishing a power of attorney. This legal document allows you to appoint someone to manage your non-trust assets if you become unable to do so yourself.

⊃ **Healthcare Power of Attorney:**
Alongside your trust and financial power of attorney, a healthcare power of attorney is a key component of a comprehensive estate plan. This document allows you to designate someone to make medical decisions on your behalf should you become incapacitated.

The Trust Document:
A REFLECTION OF YOUR WISHES

With your attorney's help, your trust document will become a detailed and clear reflection of your wishes regarding your estate. It's not just a legal formality; it's a personalized blueprint for how you want your assets to be handled and who will benefit from them. This collaboration ensures your trust is not only legally sound but also a true representation of your legacy.

Laying a Strong Legal Foundation

Collaborating with an attorney to draft your trust document is about laying a strong legal foundation for your estate plan. It's an investment in peace of mind, knowing your trust is not only compliant with legal standards but also a true embodiment of your wishes and goals for your legacy. This step is crucial in ensuring your trust functions as intended, providing security and clarity for both you and your beneficiaries.

Determining the Assets to Include in Your Trust:
A DETAILED CONSIDERATION

In the process of establishing a trust, one of the most critical steps is determining which assets to include. This decision is pivotal in shaping how your trust will function and serve your estate planning goals. Let's delve deeper into the nuances of selecting the right assets for your trust.

Variety of Assets for Trust Inclusion

Cash and Equivalents: These are the simplest assets to include in a trust and can cover anything from bank account balances to money market funds. They provide liquidity and ease of management within the trust.

- **Real Estate:**
  Including real estate in your trust can be advantageous, especially for avoiding probate. However, if the property is mortgaged, transferring it into a trust might require consent from the lender, and in some cases, the transfer might trigger a due-on-sale clause.

- **Investments:**
  Stocks, bonds, mutual funds, and other investment accounts are common assets for a trust. They can help in growing the trust's value over time and provide financial benefits to the beneficiaries.

- **Business Interests:**
  If you own a business or have interests in partnerships or limited liability companies, including these in your trust can ensure smooth succession and management continuity.

➲ **Personal Property:**
Valuables like art, jewelry, antiques, and collectibles can also be included. These items often carry not just financial value but emotional significance, making their inclusion important for many trustors.

Assets to Approach with Caution

➲ **Mortgaged Property:**
Transferring a mortgaged property into a trust can be complex and may require specific lender consent or trigger a due-on-sale clause, necessitating careful legal and financial consultation.

➲ **Financial Accounts:**
While regular checking or savings accounts used for daily expenses can be included in a trust for management simplicity, it's important to consider how this aligns with your broader financial and estate planning goals.

➲ **Retirement Accounts:**
Generally, it's not advisable to transfer retirement accounts like IRAs and 401(k)s into a trust due to tax implications. Instead, consider naming the trust as a beneficiary of these accounts.

➲ **Medical Savings Accounts:**
These accounts usually have tax advantages that might be compromised if they are included in a trust. Like retirement accounts, they can instead name the trust as a beneficiary.

➲ **Life Insurance:**
While life insurance can be included in a trust, doing so might have estate tax implications. It's often more strategic to name the trust as the beneficiary of the policy.

⊃ **Vehicles:**
  Cars, boats, and other vehicles can be included, but be aware of the potential for estate taxes and depreciation. Each state has different rules regarding vehicles in trusts, so local legal advice is crucial.

Determining which assets to include in your trust is a process that requires careful thought and often, professional guidance. Each asset type brings its own set of benefits and considerations. The key is to align your asset selection with your overall estate planning objectives, ensuring your trust effectively captures your financial legacy and serves the intended purpose for your beneficiaries. Remember, the assets you choose to include in your trust are more than just items of financial value; they represent the legacy you wish to leave behind and the careful planning you've done to secure your family's future.

Conclusion

Creating a trust is a deeply personal and strategic endeavor that requires careful consideration of various factors. From selecting the type of trust that aligns with your goals to determining the assets to include, choosing a successor trustee, identifying beneficiaries, and setting clear trust rules, every step is crucial in ensuring your trust effectively captures your intentions and secures your legacy.

As we've explored, the type of trust you choose will significantly influence how your assets are managed and distributed. Whether opting for a revocable trust for its flexibility or an irrevocable trust for its tax benefits and asset protection, the decision should reflect your specific financial landscape and estate planning objectives. Additionally, the thoughtful selection of assets, the designation of a responsible successor trustee, and the establishment of clear, adaptable rules are all pivotal in crafting a trust that stands the test of time and honors your legacy.

The benefits of collaboration with an experienced estate planning attorney can't be overstated. Their expertise ensures your trust document is not only legally sound but also a true reflection of your wishes and goals. This foundation sets the stage for the next critical phase in the trust creation process: funding your trust.

With the structure of your trust established, the next essential phase is to fund it—transforming your plan into action by integrating your assets with your objectives. In the upcoming chapter, we will delve into the strategies for asset allocation and management to enhance the effectiveness and privacy of your trust.

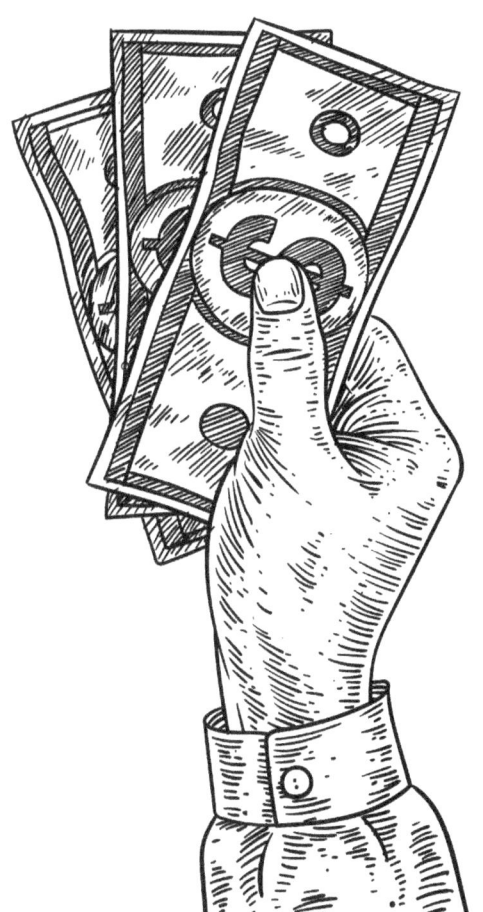

Chapter 4

Funding the Trust:
Asset Allocation Strategies

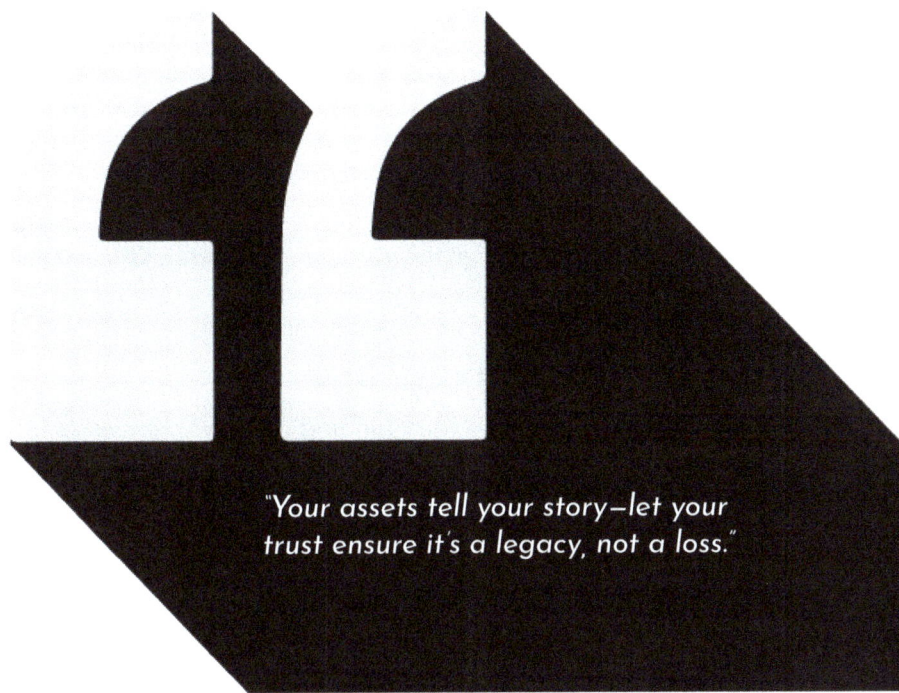

"Your assets tell your story—let your trust ensure it's a legacy, not a loss."

Transitioning from the creation of your trust to its funding is a natural progression in the estate planning journey. While crafting a trust is about envisioning and documenting your legacy, funding the trust brings that vision to life by ensuring your assets are properly aligned with your estate planning objectives. This chapter delves into the nuances of this pivotal phase, highlighting essential strategies for asset allocation that enhance both privacy and the efficient management of your estate.

The Importance of Privacy and Proper Trust Funding

One significant benefit of a revocable trust is the privacy it offers. High-profile cases involving celebrity estate disputes highlight the potential public exposure and conflicts that can result from inadequate estate planning, issues revocable trusts can help mitigate by keeping estate matters out of the probate process. Unlike wills, which undergo probate and thus become matters of public record, the contents and provisions of your trust remain confidential. This secrecy not only protects the privacy of your estate but also safeguards its integrity from the probate process. Consequently, meticulous trust funding is paramount to bypass probate, thereby preserving the estate's confidentiality and its assets' seamless transition.

Step 1: Asset Inventory

The foundation of effective trust funding is a comprehensive inventory of your assets. This inventory should encompass both tangible assets, such as real estate and personal property, and intangible ones, including bank accounts, investments, and life insurance policies. A thorough understanding of your assets is crucial to developing a strong funding strategy for your trust. This initial step lays the groundwork for a systematic approach to allocating which assets will be included in the trust.

Step 2: Legal Foundations

Establishing your trust on a solid legal basis cannot be overstated. Working with an experienced estate planning attorney is essential to tailor your trust documents to your specific needs and goals. This collaboration ensures your estate planning efforts are both legally sound and effective, providing a sturdy framework for your trust and aligning with your estate planning objectives.

Step 3: Asset Transfers and Strategic Funding

A sophisticated understanding of how to fund your trust is critical, given the varied nature of assets. This step involves not only the technical process of transferring assets but also emphasizes a strategic focus on ensuring these transfers are handled with precision. For real estate and tangible assets, transferring them into the trust may require deed re-titling and potentially discussions with mortgage lenders to align the ownership records with the trust structure. For financial instruments such as bank accounts and investment portfolios, updating account titles and beneficiary designations is necessary, listing the trust as the primary or contingent beneficiary. This ensures these assets are properly incorporated into the trust without legal hiccups.

7. Table of Asset Categories

Asset Type	Liquidity	Growth Potential	Suitability for Trusts	Notes
Real Estate	Low	High	Very Suitable	Best in irrevocable trusts for estate tax benefits.
Business Interests	Low-Medium	High	Suitable	Requires proper structuring to maintain control.
Investments (Stocks, Bonds, etc.)	High	High	Very Suitable	Ideal for revocable and irrevocable trusts.
Personal Property (Jewelry, Collectibles, etc.)	Medium	Low-Medium	Less Suitable	May be subject to personal use restrictions.

The process must adhere to the detailed instructions outlined in your trust documents, with each type of asset demanding a specific strategy for inclusion. Collaborating closely with your attorney during this phase is vital to ensure all asset transfers are conducted accurately and comply with legal standards. This strategic approach ensures the trust is not only legally sound but also fully equipped to manage your assets efficiently, reflecting your estate planning objectives and ultimately preserving your legacy.

Step 4: Regular Updates and Maintenance

Funding your trust is an ongoing process, not a one-time task. Regular reviews and updates of the trust are essential to ensure it accurately reflects significant life events, like marriage, childbirth, divorce, or new asset acquisitions, thereby maintaining its relevance and effectiveness. Consistent maintenance ensures the trust remains relevant and operational, accurately reflecting your current circumstances and wishes.

Step 5: Education and Empowerment

Gaining a deep understanding of the trust funding process is empowering. By familiarizing yourself with the involved procedures and the implications of various funding strategies, you can make knowledgeable decisions that enhance the benefits of your estate plan. This knowledge enables effective collaboration with legal advisors and proactive engagement in your estate planning journey.

Tailoring the Trust Funding Process

Each trust is a reflection of the trustor's unique financial situation and personal objectives. Customizing the funding process to suit individual needs not only meets legal prerequisites but also perfectly aligns with the trustor's vision and goals.

Navigating Complex Asset Transfers

For assets that present more intricate considerations, such as business interests or intellectual property, the funding process demands careful planning and coordination. It is crucial to work with specialized legal and financial advisors to effectively navigate these complexities, ensuring all transfers are compliant and strategically sound.

Ongoing Management and Adaptation

As your life and financial landscape evolve, so too should your trust. The dynamic nature of your financial and personal life necessitates your trust adapts over time.

Regularly reviewing and adjusting the trust ensures it continues to fulfill its purpose effectively, accommodating any changes in your asset base or personal circumstances.

Conclusion:
THE ART OF EFFECTIVE TRUST FUNDING

Mastering the art of trust funding is indispensable, particularly in the African American and other minority communities, where strategic estate planning is a vital component of wealth preservation and legacy building. This chapter has explored the comprehensive process of trust funding, emphasizing the significance of meticulous planning, legal expertise, and proactive management. By focusing on the unique characteristics of each asset, customizing the funding process to individual preferences, and adapting to life's changes, your trust can serve as a powerful instrument for securing long-term financial health and crafting a lasting legacy for generations to come.

Now that your trust is funded and your estate plan is taking shape, it's vital to consider the role of taxation. Understanding the tax implications of your decisions can help safeguard your assets and ensure a smoother transfer of wealth. The next chapter delves into the intersection of trusts and taxes, offering strategies to protect your legacy from unnecessary financial burdens.

Chapter 5

Trust and Taxation:
A Comprehensive Guide to the
Implications for Revocable Trusts

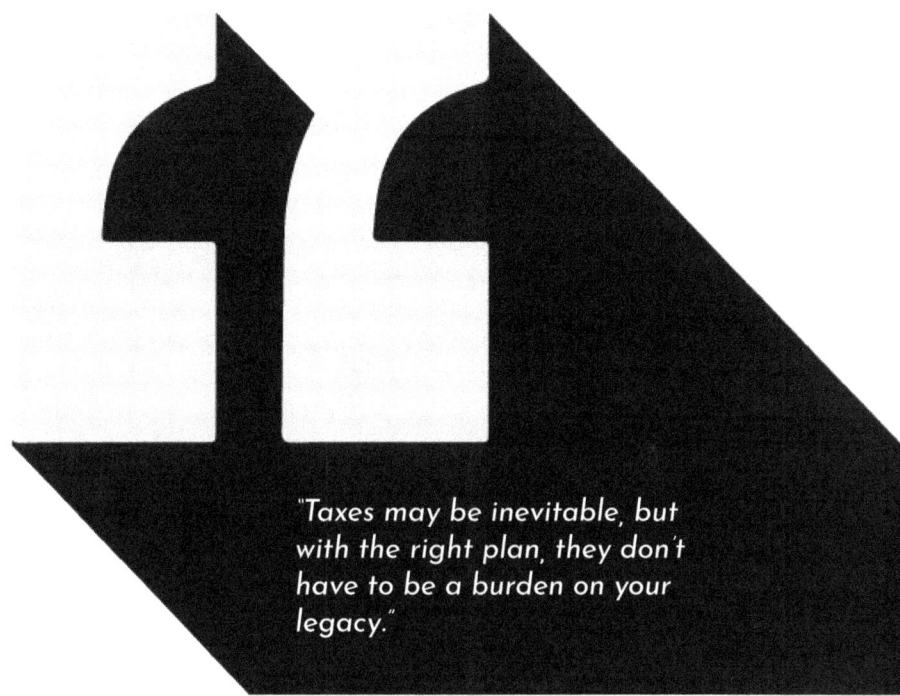

"Taxes may be inevitable, but with the right plan, they don't have to be a burden on your legacy."

"There's only three things that's for sure: taxes, death, and trouble." Marvin Gaye's words from his iconic song "Trouble Man" resonate just as profoundly today as they did when he first sang them. As a Pentecostal PK (preacher's kid) and a lifelong fan of Marvin's music, I've often pondered the deeper significance of that line. It's a stark reminder that, regardless of our status or wealth, these are the constants we all face.

The lives of celebrities like Michael Jackson, Prince, James Brown, and Aretha Franklin offer clear examples of the financial "trouble" that arises from inadequate tax planning in estate management. Despite their towering legacies and substantial wealth, each of these legends' estates encountered significant tax and legal complications after their deaths. Michael Jackson's estate, for instance, faced years of legal battles over the IRS's valuation of his assets. Meanwhile, Prince, Aretha Franklin, and James Brown left estates mired in probate and tax disputes, delaying the distribution of their wealth to their rightful heirs.

Most of us may not have assets as complex to distribute as these icons, but we can certainly benefit from preparing for tax implications in our own estate planning. Proper planning ensures our families are spared unnecessary hardships and our legacies are preserved.

Welcome to an enlightening exploration of the intersecting worlds of trust and taxation. This chapter delves into the intersection of taxes and revocable trusts, providing a comprehensive guide to help you navigate these complexities. By understanding the intricacies of tax implications, you can take control of your legacy, make informed decisions that will secure your family's financial future, and ensure they avoid unnecessary hardships when the inevitable comes.

The Historical Context of Tax and Inheritance in the African American Community

To fully appreciate the significance of proper tax planning, it is essential to acknowledge the historical context that has shaped the understanding of taxes within certain communities, including the African American community. Historically, many African American families have experienced the loss of their family's property due to challenges associated with taxes and inheritance. The concept of heirs' property, where property ownership is shared amongst multiple family members without clear legal documentation, has often resulted in the loss of family land and assets for taxes. This issue has been compounded by the lack of access to proper legal and financial advice, which has left many families vulnerable to losing their hard-earned assets. As a result, African American families have become acutely aware of the negative repercussions of not properly addressing their tax responsibilities.

The Johnson Family and the Power of Revocable Trusts

We'll illustrate these complexities through the fictional, yet realistic, story of the Johnson family. The Johnsons, owners of a substantial real estate portfolio, were confronted with a typical question: how could they transfer these properties to their children without incurring hefty taxes, especially capital gains tax? Their goal was to preserve their wealth for future generations while minimizing tax liabilities. After consulting financial planners and estate planning attorneys, they chose to place their properties into a revocable living trust. This strategic move aimed to avoid the lengthy and expensive probate process, preserving the full value of the properties for their children.

A key advantage of using a revocable trust is that it facilitates a step-up in basis for capital gains tax purposes upon the death of the trustor. When the trustor passes away, the properties held within the trust receive a step-up in basis to their fair market value at the time of death. This effectively minimizes or eliminates the capital gains tax that would be due if the beneficiaries decide to sell the properties soon after the transfer. This aspect of estate planning is crucial for the Johnsons, ensuring a more tax-efficient transfer of wealth to their children.

Key Tax Implications of Revocable Trusts

A determining factor in their decision was understanding that moving properties into a trust is not viewed as a sale, thus, it doesn't trigger capital gains tax. However, the tax implications did not end there. As is common with many families utilizing a revocable trust, all income generated by the trust's assets like rental income from their properties, would need to be declared on their personal income tax returns. This ensures the family remains compliant with tax laws while still benefiting from the income generated by their properties.

Importantly, incorporating real estate into a revocable trust did not affect their property tax obligations. This was a relief for the Johnsons, as local tax laws generally do not impose additional property taxes due to such transfers. While revocable trusts do not directly reduce estate taxes, they can be designed in a way that optimizes estate tax liabilities. This was a notable consideration for the Johnsons, whose estate value was substantial. The assets within the trust are included in the grantor's taxable estate, but with strategic estate planning, revocable trusts can be tailored to optimize estate tax liabilities, particularly for estates that exceed federal estate tax exemptions.

Again one significant advantage of the trust was the avoidance of probate. This led to a more efficient transfer of their properties to their children, potentially saving on probate fees and speeding up the process for beneficiaries to access their inheritance. The avoidance of probate also helps maintain privacy, as probate proceedings are public records, while trusts remain private documents. This advantage is significant, providing families with the peace of mind their assets will be transferred efficiently, in line with their desires.

As we previously discussed, beyond real estate, revocable trusts can also encompass other assets, such as insurance policies and bank accounts. Life insurance policies, when included in a revocable trust, enable a more controlled distribution of the death benefit. This control can be particularly beneficial in managing how beneficiaries receive and use these funds. Transferring life insurance policies into a trust typically does not incur immediate tax consequences, but it's essential to understand the policy's terms and any potential impact on the insurance benefits.

Bank accounts, including savings and money market accounts, can also be incorporated into a revocable trust. This integration simplifies asset management and ensures these funds are distributed according to the trust's terms. For income taxation, the income generated by these accounts, such as interest, is reported on the grantor's personal income tax return, as the trust is considered an extension of the grantor. This transparency simplifies the tax reporting process for the Johnsons, avoiding the need for separate income tax reporting for the trust.

Homeowners may also have concerns about real estate and mortgages when considering a revocable trust. Transferring real estate into a revocable trust is primarily aimed at avoiding probate, but homeowners may worry about triggering mortgage issues, such as the "due-on sale" clause. Federal laws, however, protect homeowners who transfer their primary residence into a revocable trust, as long as they continue to reside there. This offers reassurance their mortgage terms will remain unaffected by the transfer.

Revocable trusts offer a practical and flexible solution for managing assets efficiently and crafting a legacy that aligns with personal goals and adapts to changing family dynamics. While they do not significantly reduce tax liabilities during the grantor's lifetime, the benefits of probate avoidance, cost reduction, and controlled asset distribution make them an attractive option. However, maximizing these benefits requires a proper understanding of the trust's tax implications. Assistance from legal and financial experts can be invaluable in this regard, ensuring the trust is structured to align with tax laws and the family's goals.

In conclusion, the story of the Johnsons exemplifies the need for careful consideration and strategic planning in trust and taxation planning. These considerations are not just about legal compliance and asset distribution, but also about making informed decisions that preserve a family's legacy and pass it on according to their wishes. Revocable trusts, while complex, offer a powerful means of estate planning when approached with a thorough understanding and strategic planning.

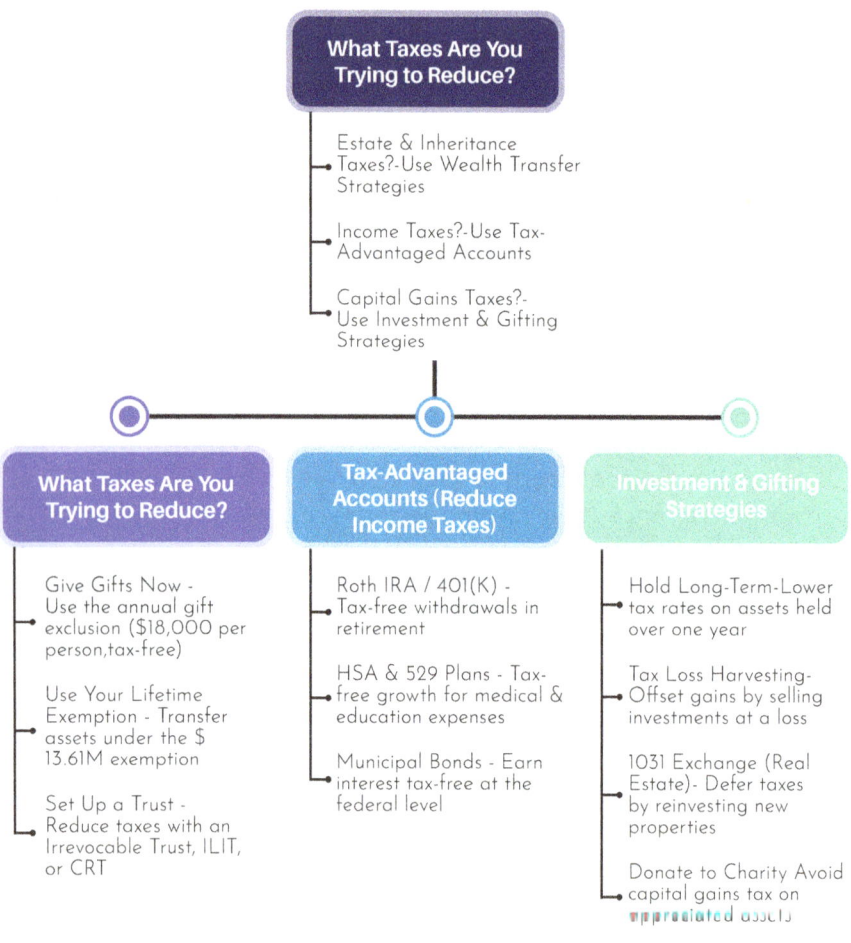

Chapter 6

Comprehensive Tax Strategies for Trusts

"The key to financial security isn't just earning wealth—it's understanding how to protect it from erosion."

Understanding the taxation of trusts is crucial for effective estate planning. This chapter provides an overview of the various tax rules and implications that can affect trusts, offering insights into managing assets efficiently while complying with tax requirements. While not all tax rules may apply to every reader, this chapter aims to provide a broad understanding of the diverse tax considerations involved, equipping readers with the foundational knowledge needed to navigate the complexities of trust taxation.

1. Income Taxation of Trusts

Overview of Trust Taxation

Trusts, as legal entities, are subject to specific taxation rules that vary significantly based on their structure and the relationship between the trustor (the person who creates the trust) and the beneficiary. The Internal Revenue Service (IRS) distinguishes between different types of trusts primarily based on their ability to be altered or revoked by the grantor. These distinctions have profound implications for how trusts are taxed, particularly concerning income generated by trust assets.

Grantor Trust Rules

For revocable trusts, where the grantor retains control and the ability to alter the trust's terms, the IRS applies what are known as the "grantor trust rules." Under these rules, for tax purposes, the grantor is considered the owner of the trust's assets. Consequently, all income generated by these assets—be it capital gains, dividends, or interest—is reported directly on the grantor's personal income tax return. This approach simplifies the tax reporting process but also places the full burden of tax liabilities on the grantor. The key benefit here is the simplicity in management and taxation, as it avoids the need for the trust to file a separate tax return.

Non-Grantor Trusts

In contrast, if a trust becomes irrevocable—meaning the grantor has relinquished all control and cannot alter its terms—it may be treated as a separate taxable entity. Generally, these trusts are required to file their own tax return using IRS Form 1041, although there are specific circumstances and exceptions that can affect this requirement. Non-grantor trusts are taxed on any income they retain, while distributions to beneficiaries are typically taxed at the beneficiaries' personal income tax rates. Managing a non-grantor trust requires careful planning to optimize tax implications, particularly with respect to distributions and the timing of income recognition.

2. Estate Tax Considerations

Unified Credit and Exemptions

A critical aspect of estate planning involves understanding how to leverage the unified credit and applicable estate tax exemptions. These mechanisms are designed to minimize the estate tax burden upon the grantor's death. The unified credit effectively allows a significant portion of the estate to be passed on to heirs without incurring federal estate taxes. For 2023, the federal estate tax exemption is set at $12.06 million per individual, meaning that estates valued below this threshold are not subject to federal estate taxes. Strategic use of this exemption, especially in planning the timing and nature of trust funding, can significantly reduce the taxable estate's size. It is important to note that state estate tax implications can differ from federal regulations and are discussed below.

Portability

The concept of portability further enhances the strategic use of exemptions. Portability allows the surviving spouse to utilize any unused portion of their deceased spouse's federal estate tax exemption. This means that with proper estate planning, couples can effectively shield double the amount of the exemption from federal estate taxes, protecting more of their wealth for future generations. To activate this benefit, timely filing of an estate tax return upon the first spouse's death is crucial, even if no tax is due.

3. Gift Tax Implications

Annual Exclusion

Gifts made to trusts can also engage the gift tax rules, which allow for an annual exclusion from gift tax. For 2023, the annual gift tax exclusion is $17,000 per recipient. This means that a grantor can transfer up to $17,000 annually to as many individuals as they wish, or trusts, without these gifts reducing their lifetime gift tax exemption or requiring the filing of a gift tax return. When structured properly, such as ensuring the trust provides beneficiaries with certain rights to the gifted assets (like the right to withdraw), these transfers can qualify for the annual exclusion.

Lifetime Exclusion

Beyond the annual exclusion, larger transfers might tap into the grantor's lifetime gift tax exemption. This exemption mirrors the estate tax exemption, allowing a total of $12.06 million to be given away during the grantor's lifetime without incurring gift tax. Strategic use of this lifetime exemption can be particularly effective in estate planning, allowing the grantor to reduce the size of their estate while spreading wealth during their lifetime.

4. Generation-Skipping Transfer Tax (GSTT)

GSTT Overview

The Generation-Skipping Transfer Tax (GSTT) is an additional tax that applies to transfers to individuals who are at least two generations below the grantor, such as grandchildren. The purpose of the GSTT is to prevent the avoidance of estate taxes across multiple generations. This tax is levied in addition to any gift or estate tax and can significantly impact the cost of passing wealth to future generations.

Strategies for Minimizing GSTT

Effective planning can leverage several strategies to minimize the impact of GSTT. One common approach is the establishment of a generation-skipping trust (GST), which can hold assets in trust for multiple generations without incurring GSTT at each generational transfer. The trust's assets can grow and benefit descendants without repeated taxation, under certain limits known as the GST exemption amount—identical to the federal estate tax exemption. Strategic allocation of this exemption and perhaps even annual gifting strategies that utilize the GSTT exemption can protect significant amounts of wealth from taxes over generations.

5. Charitable Trusts and Deductions

Benefits of Charitable Trusts

Incorporating charitable giving within estate planning cannot only fulfill philanthropic goals but also provide substantial tax benefits. Charitable trusts, such as Charitable Remainder Trusts (CRTs) and Charitable Lead Trusts (CLTs), are two prevalent types used to integrate charity into estate and tax planning effectively. These trusts allow for income and estate tax deductions, based on the value of the assets passed to charity, and can be structured to provide income streams to beneficiaries for a term of years or for life.

Types of Charitable Trusts

◒ **Charitable Remainder Trusts (CRTs):**
CRTs allow the grantor to receive an income stream for a period determined by the trust (either the grantor's lifetime or a fixed term, not exceeding twenty years), after which the remainder of the trust assets go to designated charities. This setup provides an immediate income tax deduction based on the present value of the charitable remainder.

◒ **Charitable Lead Trusts (CLTs)**
In contrast, CLTs provide an income stream to one or more charities for a term of years, with the remainder of the assets eventually returning to the grantor or passing to the beneficiaries. This structure allows for estate or gift tax deductions on the value of the income stream provided to the charity.

6. State Tax Considerations

Variability in State Laws

When planning trusts, it's crucial to consider not only federal but also state tax implications. Some states levy their own estate or inheritance taxes, which can significantly differ from federal tax laws. States like New York, Massachusetts, and Oregon, for instance, have estate taxes, while others like New Jersey and Pennsylvania impose inheritance taxes, which are based on the relationship to the decedent.

Planning for State Taxes

Strategies to mitigate state tax liabilities might include establishing trusts in states with favorable tax laws or restructuring the ownership of assets to minimize exposure to multiple state tax regimes. Understanding the specific tax landscape of the state(s) in which the grantor and beneficiaries reside, or where the trust holds substantial property, is essential. This knowledge ensures the trust is not only crafted to comply with federal tax laws but also optimized to minimize potential state tax liabilities.

7. Trustee Responsibilities and Liabilities

Fiduciary Duties

Trustees play a crucial role in the management of a trust. As fiduciaries, they are legally obligated to act in the best interest of the trust beneficiaries. This includes prudently investing trust assets, ensuring the trust complies with all applicable tax laws, and administering the trust according to its terms. The trustee's responsibilities are not only managerial but also involve significant legal and ethical obligations to maintain the trust's integrity and purpose.

Potential Liabilities

Trustees must also handle potential liabilities that can arise from their management roles. Failure to comply with fiduciary duties can lead to legal consequences, including personal liability for losses incurred by the trust. Effective risk management, often supported by legal counsel, is essential to protect trustees from potential claims and to ensure they fulfill their roles without error or oversight.

8. Administrative Costs and Professional Fees

Costs Overview

Establishing and maintaining a trust involves various administrative and professional fees. These can include legal fees for drafting and updating trust documents, accounting fees for annual tax filing and audits, and possibly trustee fees if a professional trustee is involved. These costs should be factored into the overall estate planning strategy to ensure the benefits of having the trust justify the expenses.

Cost Management

It is possible to manage these costs through careful planning and by choosing the right professionals. For example, selecting a trustee who can handle both administrative and investment responsibilities might reduce the need for outside consultants. Additionally, periodic reviews of the trust's operations can help identify areas where expenses can be minimized without compromising the trust's effectiveness.

9. Tax Law Changes

Staying Informed

Tax laws are dynamic and can change due to legislative, regulatory, or judicial developments. Staying informed about these changes is crucial for trustees and grantors alike to ensure the trust remains compliant and continues to serve its intended purpose efficiently. This might involve regular consultations with tax professionals or legal advisors who specialize in estate planning and trust management.

Adapting to New Laws

When tax laws change, it may be necessary to adjust the trust structure or its operations to maintain its efficacy and tax efficiency. This could involve anything from restructuring the investment strategy to amending the trust document itself. Proactive adaptation to tax law changes can protect the trust's assets from increased liability and ensure its benefits continue to align with the grantor's intentions.

Additional Considerations

International Tax Issues

Trusts that involve non-U.S. persons as grantors, trustees, or beneficiaries, or that hold foreign assets, face additional complexities. International tax treaties, foreign tax credits, and compliance with the reporting requirements of multiple jurisdictions are critical considerations that require specialized expertise.

Conclusion

Effective trust management and tax planning require a comprehensive understanding of myriad factors that can influence a trust's operation and efficacy. As you navigate these complexities, it becomes increasingly important to engage with professional advisors who can provide tailored insights and guidance. By considering the detailed aspects of trust taxation—from income and estate tax implications to administrative costs and evolving laws—trustees and grantors are better positioned to make informed decisions that safeguard and enhance the value of the trust's assets. This strategic approach not only ensures legal compliance and fiscal responsibility but also fulfills the ultimate goal of preserving and passing on a lasting legacy in accordance with the grantor's wishes. Engaging knowledgeable professionals can illuminate the path forward, helping to translate intricate legal and tax considerations into actionable steps that secure your trust's enduring success.

As we transition to the next chapter, we will explore the essential roles and responsibilities of trustees and beneficiaries, ensuring that every element of your trust aligns with your overarching vision for generational wealth and harmony.

14. Case Study Walkthrough of Tax Strategies

STEP-1 — A — Identifying the Tax Challenges

STEP-2 — B — Implementing Tax Strategies

STEP-3 — C — Final Outcomes

Estate Tax Concern - Their estate exceeds the federal estate tax exemption ($13.61M in 2024), but if it grows, their heirs may face a hefty tax bill.

Income Tax on Investments - Their portfolio generates taxable investment income.

Capital Gains on Real Estate - Their portfolio generates taxable investment income.

Lifetime Gifting - They gift $18,000 per year to each of their two children, reducing their taxable estate.

Irrevocable Trust - They transfer $3 million of investments into an Irrevocable Life Insurance Trust (ILIT) to cover future estate taxes.

Charitable Remainder Trust (CRT) - They donate a highly appreciated stock portfolio, receive a charitable deduction, and still earn income for life.

1031 Exchange for Real Estate - They donate a highly appreciated stock portfolio, receive a charitable deduction, and still earn income for life.

Estate tax reduced by 35% through gifting and trusts.

Charitable donations lower taxable income while supporting causes they care about.

Heirs receive more wealth with less tax burden.

Comparison of before-and-after tax implications

Before tax implications	VS	After tax implications
$10M taxable estate	**Estate Tax Exposure**	Reduced taxable estate to $6.5M
$500K taxable gain	**Capital Gains on Stocks**	Avoided via CRT
$80K/year taxable	**Income Tax on Investments**	Lowered via tax-advantaged accounts
$1M taxable gain	**Real Estate Capital Gains**	Deferred via 1031 Exchange

Chapter 7

Estate Planning as a Family Conversation—Understanding the Roles of Trustees and Beneficiaries

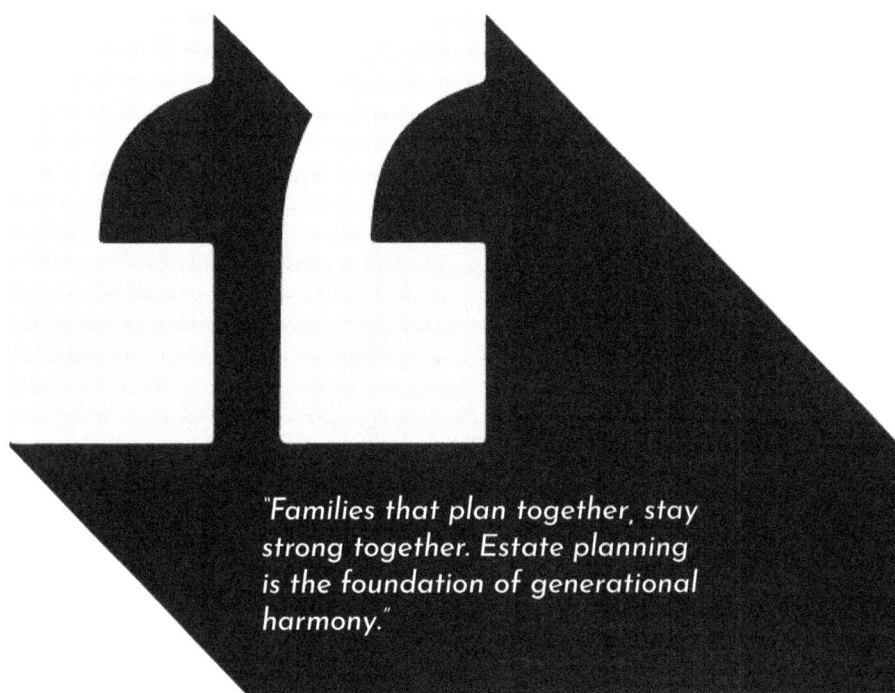

"Families that plan together, stay strong together. Estate planning is the foundation of generational harmony."

At the heart of our discussion in this chapter are the intricate and sensitive dynamics of family relationships, particularly in the context of estate planning. The African American community deeply cherishes family bonds, and the relationships formed therein. They are our most precious treasures. However, the challenge lies in thinking about resources—who gets what, who controls what, and how these decisions affect our relationships.

These types of conversations are difficult, even more so when concerns are voiced and issues remain unresolved. It's an uncomfortable reality, but it's a necessary step towards establishing a legacy and catalyzing change. By embracing this challenge, we have the opportunity to change the trajectory of our people—one person, one family, one community at a time. By overcoming the taboo surrounding discussions about wealth, we can face our fears, change old patterns, and move towards creating stability, a legacy, and generational wealth.

I've had the privilege of witnessing many families muster the courage to change and take proactive steps towards estate planning. In this chapter, I will share several hypothetical scenarios that mirror many of the situations I've encountered.

Let's examine the case of the Jones family. The family is composed of two parents and three children—two daughters, and a son. The oldest (a son) and the youngest (a daughter) have struggled to find their footing in life. Mr. and Mrs. Jones, in their wisdom, recognize the unique strengths and weaknesses of their children. They have decided to designate their middle daughter as the successor trustee and the executor of their wills.

The task at hand is to communicate this decision to their other two children in a way that prevents tension during family gatherings. Mr. and Mrs. Jones are acutely aware of the potential for familial discord that this decision could stir up. However, they also understand that open, honest discussions—whether one-on-one or as a group—are crucial in navigating these complexities.

By thoughtfully selecting trustees and educating beneficiaries, families like the Joneses can ensure that their estate plans not only secure their financial legacy but also preserve the unity and bonds that are so cherished in the community. As we navigate these stories and the lessons they hold, remember, the journey towards estate planning and creating a legacy is as much about maintaining trust and harmony within the family as it is about wealth management.

In the journey of the Jones family, we glimpse the delicate equilibrium required when broaching the topic of estate planning. They grapple with the decision to appoint their middle child as the successor trustee, a choice laden with potential familial tension. Yet, this decision need not be a source of discord if approached correctly. Here are several strategies that could help facilitate this process:

⊃ **1. Individual Conversations:**
The Joneses might opt for one-on-one discussions, allowing them to shape their conversations according to each child's emotional maturity and comprehension level. This tailored approach could alleviate some of the apprehension surrounding their decision.

⊃ **2. Open Family Dialogue:**
Another approach is to foster an open family dialogue where the Joneses discuss their estate plan as a collective. This strategy, though challenging, promotes understanding by focusing on the reasoning behind their decision and its significance for the family's future.

⊃ **3. Professional Mediation:**
Engaging an external advisor such as an estate planning attorney can offer a neutral perspective, aiding in navigating these tough discussions.

The trustee's selection is a task that demands careful consideration. The trustee must be trustworthy, financially competent, and capable of handling complex affairs. For the Jones family, their middle child possesses these qualities, making her an appropriate choice. However, the key to maintaining harmony lies in effectively communicating this decision to her and the rest of the family.

15. Family Dynamics and Trust Roles Diagram

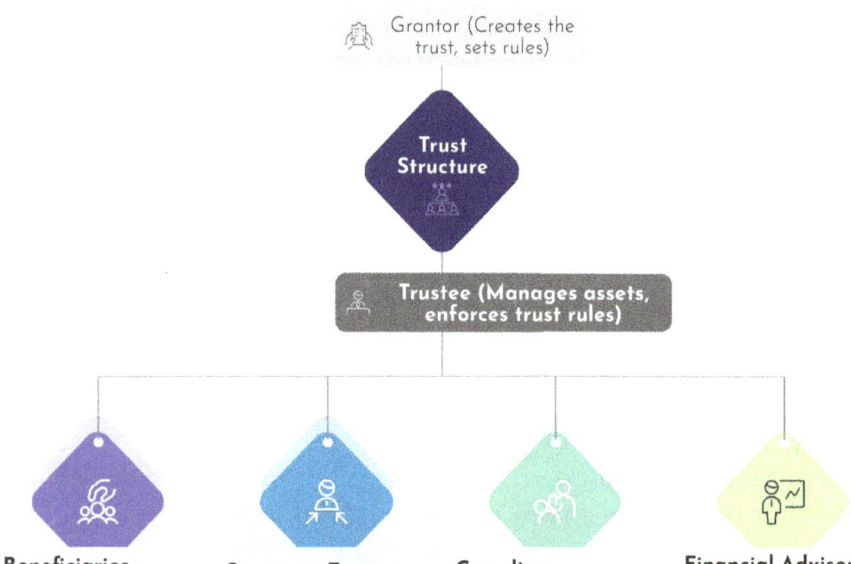

Beneficiaries
Individuals or entities who receive assets or benefits from the trust.

Successor Trustee
A backup trustee who takes over in case of incapacity or passing of the original trustee

Guardian
If minor children are involved, the guardian ensures their financial needs are met.

Financial Advisor
Helps manage trust assets for long-term growth and sustainability. Diagram Structure.

It's important to note that a revocable trust typically becomes irrevocable upon the grantor's death, thrusting the successor trustee into a role that requires understanding and adherence to the trust's terms. For the Joneses' middle child, this means managing the trust according to its stipulations.

Trustees must uphold the highest standards of asset management and legal compliance. They should be adept at managing various assets, aligning their actions with the trust's objectives, and maintaining regular communication with beneficiaries. This transparency is integral to establishing understanding and unity about the process within the family.

Beneficiaries need to be educated about the trust's role, purpose, and their rights within it. Such clarity can preempt misunderstandings and conflicts, promoting confidence and transparency in the estate planning process.

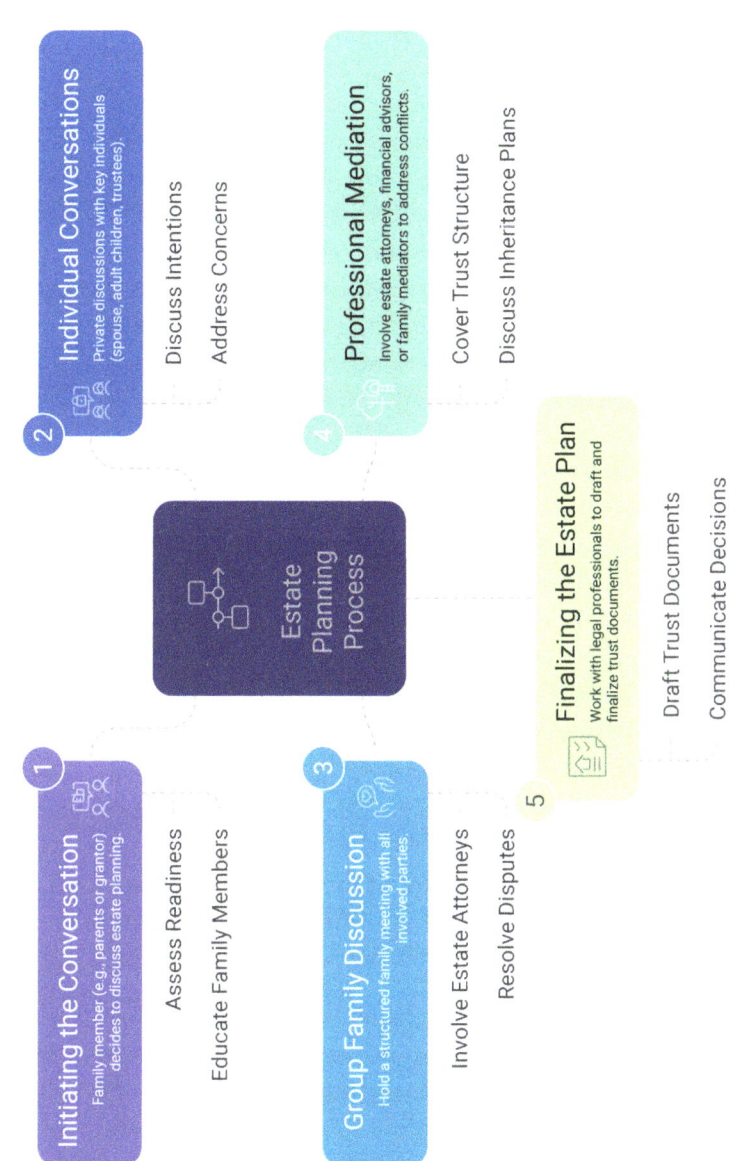

16. Flowchart of the Trust Discussion Process

The Jones family's story encapsulates many of the challenges African American families face in estate planning. Open, honest discussions—whether individually or as a group—are essential in navigating these complexities. By thoughtfully selecting trustees and educating beneficiaries, families can ensure that their estate plans secure their financial legacy while preserving the unity and bonds so cherished in our community.

As we transition into discussing beneficiaries, it's crucial to consider the need to protect some beneficiaries from themselves. This can be a sensitive topic, but addressing it is necessary to ensure the longevity of the estate and support its intended impact. Next, we'll delve into strategies to approach this aspect of estate planning, ensuring the preservation of wealth across generations while safeguarding the interests and well-being of all beneficiaries.

Now we will address a common concern many families face when it comes to estate planning. Let's take a look at the Smith family as an example. Ms. Smith, a self-made woman who built a successful career from scratch while raising two children as a single mother has overcome numerous life challenges. Her efforts allowed her to create a solid upper-middle-class lifestyle for herself and her children.

Ms. Smith, driven by her desire to shield her children from the difficulties she faced, ensured that they had everything they needed and more. However, this protective approach had an unintended side effect: it delayed their financial maturity. Now, she finds herself worried about the possibility of her hard-earned wealth being squandered if something were to happen to her. This concern leads us to the concept of a revocable trust with a spendthrift clause.

The term "spendthrift" often evokes the image of someone who is reckless with money or has a spending problem. Although it may have a negative connotation, in the realm of estate planning, it transforms into a protective mechanism safeguarding hard-earned assets, ensuring that they serve the best interests of the intended beneficiaries and not third parties.

A spendthrift clause, commonly included in most revocable trusts, serves as a shield protecting the inheritance intended for family members or friends from creditors and other potential claimants. For someone like Ms. Smith, who is concerned about her children's financial skills, this clause offers a means to safeguard her legacy.

A trust incorporating a spendthrift clause is a specific type of trust designed to limit a beneficiary's access to its principal. Overseen by a trustee, it prevents the beneficiary's potential creditors from seizing the assets held in trust to settle a debt or other obligation.

Importantly, this protection extends to divorce proceedings. Assets held in a trust with a spendthrift clause aren't subject to equitable division in a divorce. However, once assets are distributed to the beneficiary, they can be claimed by creditors to satisfy a debt or other judgment, including equitable distribution in a divorce.

A trust with a spendthrift clause isn't only beneficial when a beneficiary is known to have spending issues. It's a protective tool that can be wielded by the grantor to safeguard the trust's assets. By appointing a non-beneficiary trustee, stronger oversight and asset protection can be achieved.

Trusts with spendthrift clauses are often used when parents want to pass assets to their family members without running the risk of those assets being claimed by the beneficiaries' creditors or lost in a divorce. This protective measure is beneficial regardless of whether any known risks exist.

Trusts with spendthrift clauses offer several benefits, including shielding the beneficiary from life's unpredictability, protecting the beneficiary from their own financial missteps, and providing financial guidance for an inexperienced beneficiary. This clause enables the trustee to control the distribution of funds, ensuring that the beneficiary doesn't squander their inheritance, effectively acting as a safeguard against both the beneficiary's potential misjudgments and third-party claims.

On the flip side, a trust without a spendthrift clause offers different benefits. In this case, beneficiaries have greater control over their inheritance and can manage it as they see fit. This can be beneficial if the beneficiaries are financially astute and capable of managing their financial affairs. However, a trust without a spendthrift clause could be more susceptible to creditors' claims, which could be a concern if the beneficiary has a history of financial instability or legal troubles.

In the case of the Smith family, Ms. Smith could weigh these options. If she believes her children are not yet prepared to prudently manage their inheritance, a trust with a spendthrift clause might be the most suitable. On the other hand, if she has confidence in her children's financial acumen and wants to afford them more freedom, a trust without a spendthrift clause could be the right choice.

The decision to include a spendthrift clause in a trust hinges on the individual circumstances of the grantor and the beneficiaries. It's a decision that must be made with a clear understanding of the benefits and drawbacks of each option, keeping in mind the need to protect beneficiaries from their own potential financial missteps and third-party claims.

Chapter Summary:

In both scenarios, *the overarching goal remains the same: to ensure the preservation of wealth across generations while safeguarding the interests and well-being of all beneficiaries. Whether through the appointment of a trusted succes-*

sor trustee or the inclusion of a protective spendthrift clause, estate planning serves as a testament to a grantor's foresight, love, and desire to provide for their loved ones even beyond their lifetime. The stories of the Jones and Smith families encapsulate the delicate balance required in estate planning within African American communities. By fostering open communication and making thoughtful decisions regarding trustees and protective clauses, families can navigate the complexities of preserving both financial legacies and cherished family bonds. These conversations, though challenging, are essential in ensuring that the wealth and unity of our families are maintained for generations to come.

As we move forward, let us bear in mind these lessons as we navigate the intricacies of estate planning, always striving for solutions that uphold each families' best interests while securing their financial futures. As we transition into the next chapter, we will explore the broader implications of living trusts and their transformative potential in wealth management and legacy building.

Chapter 8

From Vision to Reality: Effective Strategies for Managing Revocable Trusts

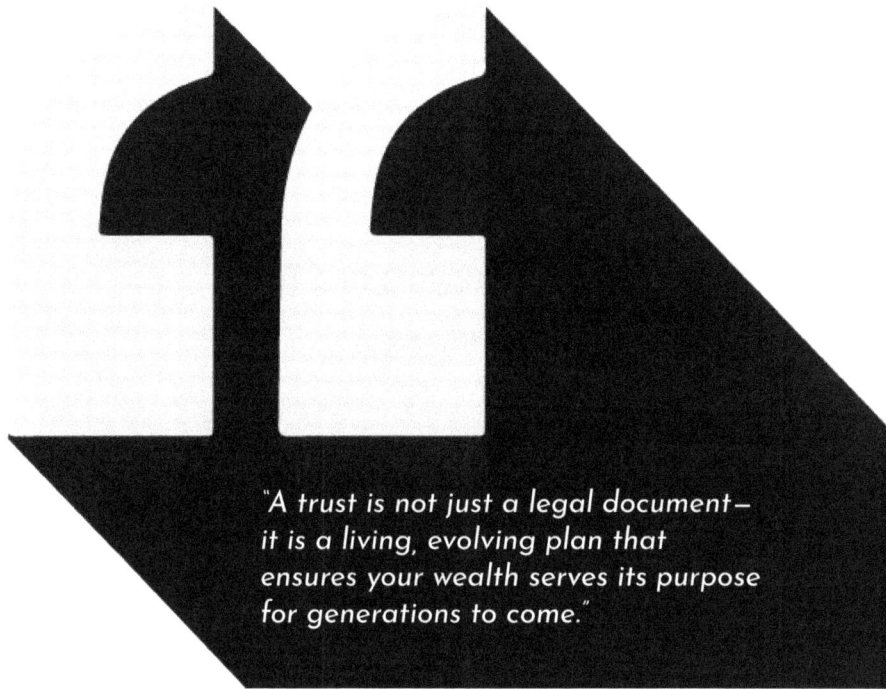

"A trust is not just a legal document—it is a living, evolving plan that ensures your wealth serves its purpose for generations to come."

In chapter 8, we review everything we have covered up until this point and synthesize it into a cohesive strategy for managing revocable trusts.

In the landscape of wealth management and legacy building, particularly within the African American community, revocable (aka living) trusts stand as powerful tools for ensuring financial security and generational success. Trusts provide a framework for passing on assets, preserving family legacies, and maintaining control over the distribution of wealth. For many families, setting up a trust represents their first encounter with formal wealth management. Seeking information and expert guidance is necessary and empowering.

Living trusts are more than just documents tucked away after signing. These legal vehicles are dynamic and evolve as life unfolds and family needs change. Their effectiveness depends on regular reviews to ensure alignment with current circumstances, from changes in family structure—such as marriages, divorces, and the birth of children—to shifts in financial or legal contexts. By proactively updating and managing your trust, you ensure it reflects your ongoing vision for the future.

17. Lifecycle of a Trust

Trust Creation

The grantor (trust creator) works with an estate attorney to establish the revocable trust. Key elements: Trust terms, trustee selection, beneficiary designation, and legal documentation.

Funding the Trust

The grantor transfers assets into the trust (real estate, bank accounts, investments, etc.). This ensures that assets avoid probate and follow trust terms after death.

Managing & Reviewing the Trust

The trustee (often the grantor) manages assets as per trust instructions. The grantor can amend or revoke the trust at any time. Regular reviews ensure alignment with financial changes, tax laws, or family needs.

Triggering Events & Transition to Successor Trustee

Upon grantor's incapacity or passing, the successor trustee takes over trust management. The successor trustee ensures assets are handled according to trust terms.

Distribution to Beneficiaries

The trustee distributes assets to beneficiaries per the trust instructions. If assets remain in trust, ongoing management continues for designated heirs.

Final Trust Closure

Once all assets are distributed, the trust is dissolved unless it's designed for long-term management (e.g., for minor children or special needs beneficiaries).

The Jackson Family:
A CASE STUDY IN STRATEGIC TRUST MANAGEMENT

To illustrate the potential power of a well-managed trust, consider the hypothetical Jackson family. Mr. and Mrs. Jackson were dedicated to building a strong financial future for their descendants, with a particular focus on preserving their family home. Their vision was realized through the creation of a revocable living trust, which would convert to an irrevocable trust upon their passing. This trust was funded with their home, rental property, and other assets, including investment accounts and life insurance policies, ensuring these resources would be used to maintain the property and provide for their descendants.

The Jacksons recognized the importance of legal expertise in achieving their goals, which led them to consulting with an estate planning attorney to ensure compliance with state regulations. They designated funds within the trust to cover the upkeep of their family home, ensuring it remained a gathering place for future generations. This foresight not only protected their assets but also created a sustainable source of family unity and pride.

Moreover, Mr. and Mrs. Jackson regularly updated their children on the trust's status and their intentions for the family estate. This proactive approach reduced potential conflict and prepared their children to manage the trust effectively, reinforcing the long-term vision for their estate planning decisions.

Funding and Asset Integration:
THE CORNERSTONE OF TRUST SUCCESS

The efficacy of any trust hinges on proper funding. This step is where many families falter, either failing to transfer all significant assets into the trust or neglecting to make new acquisitions over time. A trust must hold titles to all relevant assets—real estate, bank accounts, investment portfolios, and even personal property, like valuable artwork. This ensures that upon the death of the grantors, these assets bypass the often lengthy and costly probate process and go directly to beneficiaries according to your wishes.

Retitling assets in the name of the trust is a critical element of trust management. Without this transfer, the trust will be ineffective. Continually reviewing your asset portfolio, especially after major life events, is vital to ensuring your trust remains current. Life changes—such as purchasing a new home, acquiring additional investments, or starting a business—should trigger a review of the trust to confirm these new assets are appropriately integrated.

Record Keeping and Accountability

Once your trust is funded, maintaining detailed records becomes essential. Every asset transfer, distribution, and investment decision should be documented meticulously. This practice ensures legal compliance and provides transparency for beneficiaries and trustees. Accurate records help prevent disputes among beneficiaries and demonstrate your careful oversight.

Maintaining these records also allows the trustee to provide clear reports to beneficiaries, ensuring they are kept in the loop about the trust's management. This transparency helps build trust and understanding among all parties involved, reducing the likelihood of conflicts and misunderstandings.

Tax Implications: Navigating the Complexities

As discussed in chapters 5 and 6, tax considerations are a fundamental aspect of trust management. For revocable trusts, any gains or taxable income typically pass through to the trustor, who reports them on their individual tax returns. This allows the trustor to manage the tax burden directly. Conversely, irrevocable trusts are treated as separate tax entities, with the trust itself responsible for reporting and paying taxes on any income generated.

Consulting with a tax advisor or financial planner ensures you stay informed about your responsibilities and can implement strategies that reduce the tax burden on the trust and its beneficiaries. In the Jackson family's case, understanding the tax implications of income generated by their vacation rental property was critical to maintaining the overall health of the trust. They worked with a tax professional to ensure compliance with tax laws while taking advantage of available deductions and credits.

Transparent Communication with Beneficiaries

Trust management should never be shrouded in secrecy. Clear, transparent communication with beneficiaries can go a long way in managing expectations and preventing misunderstandings. By maintaining open lines of communication, you ensure that everyone understands the trust's purpose and the rationale behind its management. It's also helpful to outline specific expectations for how the trust should be administered after your death, allowing family members to appreciate the long-term vision behind your estate planning decisions.

Professional Management and Co-Trusteeship

As your trust grows more complex, consider bringing in professional help. In the case of the Jacksons, as their family home transitioned into a vacation rental property, they appointed an asset management company as a co-trustee. This decision allowed the trust to benefit from expert management, ensuring the property generated income while being properly maintained.

Families with substantial assets or complicated financial holdings may benefit from appointing a co-trustee or engaging the services of a corporate trustee. These professionals bring a level of oversight and objectivity that can help balance family dynamics and provide continuity in trust administration.

Professional trustees can offer specialized skills in managing complex assets, ensuring that the trust's investments are handled prudently and in accordance with the trustor's wishes. This professional management can be especially beneficial when dealing with diverse assets like businesses, rental properties, or large investment portfolios.

Continuous Learning and Adapting to Change

Trust management is not static. Laws and financial markets are continually evolving, and it's crucial to stay informed about any changes that may impact your trust. Regular consultations with estate planning attorneys and financial advisors will ensure that your trust remains compliant with the latest regulations. Beyond professional advice, consider engaging in continuous learning through workshops, literature, or financial newsletters. Being proactive about your trust management education allows you to make informed decisions that benefit both you and your beneficiaries.

The Importance of Flexibility and Adaptability

As life circumstances change, so too should your trust. Flexibility in trust management is crucial to accommodate changes in family dynamics, financial situations, and legal landscapes. Regularly revisiting and revising your trust documents ensures that they remain relevant and effective.

Consider the dynamics of the Jackson family once more. As their children grew older and their own families expanded, the needs and priorities of the trust evolved. By remaining flexible and adapting the trust to these new circumstances, the Jacksons ensured that their trust continued to serve its intended purpose.

Leveraging Technology in Trust Management

Incorporating technology into trust management can streamline processes and improve efficiency. Digital tools and platforms can help track assets, manage documentation, and facilitate communication between trustees and beneficiaries. Utilizing these technologies can make the complex task of trust management more manageable and transparent.

For example, the Jackson family could use a secure online platform to share updates and documents with their children, ensuring everyone has access to the latest information. This approach not only simplifies recordkeeping but also enhances the transparency and accessibility of the trust's management.

The Role of Education in Empowering Beneficiaries

Educating beneficiaries about the principles and practices of trust management is essential for ensuring a smooth transition of responsibilities. Providing them with the knowledge and understanding of how the trust operates and what their roles entail can prevent future conflicts and mismanagement.

In the case of the Jacksons, their proactive approach in keeping their children informed and involved in the trust's management laid the groundwork for a seamless transition. By equipping their children with the necessary knowledge, they empowered them to continue the family's legacy effectively.

Conclusion:
SHAPING A LEGACY THROUGH THOUGHTFUL TRUST MANAGEMENT

For African American families venturing into the world of trusts, understanding and implementing these strategies is essential. A living trust, managed with foresight, transparency, and professional guidance, can be a powerful tool for shaping generational legacies. The trust you establish today is not just a vehicle for passing on assets—it's a reflection of your values and a way to extend your influence far beyond your lifetime. The dedication and care you put into managing your trust today can set the foundation for financial stability and prosperity for generations to come, empowering your family with the resources and values necessary to thrive.

By synthesizing all the strategies and insights from previous chapters and incorporating new approaches such as leveraging technology and emphasizing education, you can create a robust and resilient trust. This chapter brings together all the principles and practices discussed so far, providing a comprehensive guide to effective trust management. This holistic approach ensures that your trust remains a powerful tool for achieving your long-term vision and securing your family's future.

Chapter Summary

From Vision to Reality: Effective Strategies for Managing Revocable Trusts," consolidates key insights on optimizing revocable trust management. It emphasizes the importance of regular updates to reflect changes in life and law, ensuring trusts align with the grantor's intentions. Through the Jackson family case study, the chapter illustrates effective trust management, highlighting the necessity of asset integration, diligent record-keeping, and transparent communication with beneficiaries. It also covers the roles of professional management, technology in simplifying trust processes, and education for beneficiaries to ensure smooth transitions. This chapter underscores that a well-managed trust is not just a financial tool but a legacy vehicle, extending the grantor's values and influence across generations.

Chapter 9

The Art of Legacy Letters -
A Canvas for Life's Wisdom and
Treasures Beyond Wealth

"Legacy isn't just what we leave behind—it's how we are remembered."

As we have traversed through the world of trusts and estate planning, we have deep dived into the tangible aspects of a legacy. Nonetheless, as we inch towards the end of this book, it is critical to shine a light on the intangible. A legacy letter, more than a testament to the life lived, is an enduring expression of love, wisdom, and values.

What values or lessons from your own life would you want to pass down to future generations?

The blessings of my life include not only the material opportunities I've had but also the richness of my heritage. I was fortunate to be born into a large family and live in a small town where community and connection ran deep. One of the greatest gifts was knowing not just my grandparents, but also two of my great-grandparents, along with grand uncles and aunts whose wisdom and influence were woven into my daily life.

Which family stories or traditions are most important for your loved ones to remember?

I often reflect on my grandmother, Ella Bell Cooper, who was truly a pillar of our community. A courageous woman of God, she led with both love and strength, embodying the essence of leadership not just as a pastor, but as a mother and entrepreneur. She showed me that wealth is not only in what we own, but in how we uplift those around us. Her example shaped much of my understanding of legacy—one that transcends material wealth to embrace love, wisdom, and protection.

My maternal great grandfather, Arthur Ned Richardson, was also an influence on my life. By the time I came along, it was as if wisdom spilled effortlessly from him. He was a man who valued education and hard work, and his legacy lives on through the values he imparted to our family. My father would often take me and my brother to visit his aunts and uncles—an extraordinary group of people who believed deeply in the power of education and entrepreneurship. Their names were as unique as their lives: Sun, Sterick, Noward, and Ruth. They each contributed to the rich heritage that became my inheritance, not of money, but of wisdom and principles.

My paternal grandfather, Cousby Wright, passed away before I was born. Although I never had the opportunity to meet him, his brothers, who took on fatherly roles for my father, which included imparting the strength, guidance, and wisdom that shaped our family. This created a strong sense of legacy within us, emphasizing the intangible wealth of wisdom, responsibility, and leadership. These were the true riches passed down from one generation to the next.

This chapter, inspired by the lives of my parents and my multifaceted Uncle the late Marion E. Wright, Sr., takes a turn towards understanding and embracing the holistic nature of legacy—the sum total of our material wealth, life lessons, love, and shared wisdom.

Sharing Your Knowledge:

PROVERBS 24:5 SAYS,

"The wise are mightier than the strong, and those with knowledge grow stronger and stronger." This verse highlights a fundamental truth: wisdom and knowledge are our most powerful assets. They are essential for creating and sustaining generational wealth. True wealth is not just material but also the cumulative insights from our education, relationships, experiences, and the challenges we overcome. They shape our character and decisions, and their value multiplies when shared.

In minority communities, where systemic barriers often limit access to traditional wealth, sharing knowledge is vital for survival and prosperity. Our rich tradition of oral histories—stories, wisdom, and life lessons passed down through generations—is a crucial mechanism for resilience and empowerment. This shared knowledge equips the next generation to navigate a world that may not always be welcoming or fair.

Sharing knowledge is an act of respect, acknowledging the value of those who came before us and ensuring that their lessons strengthen our communities. By passing on what we've learned, we honor our ancestors and contribute to a collective legacy. This foundation allows future generations to thrive in an ever-changing world.

Legacy Beyond Material Wealth:

In the aftermath of Bishop Marion E. Wright's homegoing celebration, my family and I were reminded that legacy transcends material wealth. It's not just about what we leave behind in tangible assets, but also the values, ideas, and wisdom we impart. Uncle Marion exemplified this in many ways. While his public life was filled with remarkable achievements in Kingdom building and community service, his true legacy encompassed much more.

Often, the demands of ministry can overshadow the personal sacrifices and contributions made to one's family. Yet, Uncle Marion managed to extend his influence well beyond his official duties. Within our family, he was a multifaceted figure—a mentor, a friend, and a safe haven. His guidance came at crucial moments, helping many of his nieces and nephews navigate the challenges of adulthood. His emotional intelligence, wit, and charm made him a pillar we could all rely on. The city where he spent most of his life, Durham, in many ways, became a launching pad for us, a testament to his unwavering support and commitment to family.

This rich tapestry of love, guidance, and emotional support that Uncle Marion wove into our lives is a powerful reminder that legacy is not confined to material wealth. He created a foundation of familial strength and emotional resilience that will shape our family for generations. This chapter delves deeper into the profound impact of legacy letters, a potent tool for sharing your life's essence with future generations. These letters ensure that the wisdom, values, and love you've cultivated continue to resonate, offering a personal touch that complements the tangible aspects of your estate.

Understanding the Essence of a Legacy Letter:

A legacy letter, often referred to as an ethical will, is a deeply personal document. It's not bound by the legalities of a typical will; instead, it's a heartfelt expression of your life's wisdom, beliefs, and experiences.

This letters your voice echoing into the future, a guidepost for those you cherish.

Legacy Letter from James Carter

February 24, 2025

Dear Family,

As I sit down to write this letter, my heart overflows with gratitude. Life has been a beautiful journey, filled with love, lessons, and moments I will cherish forever. I want you to know that each of you has brought me immense joy, and my love for you is boundless.

Values to Carry Forward

There are a few principles that have guided my life, and I hope they serve you well too:
- Kindness is never wasted. Treat people with compassion, even when it's difficult. A small act of kindness can change someone's entire day—or even their life.
- Integrity matters. Do what is right, even when no one is watching. Your character is your legacy.
- Cherish time with loved ones. In the end, the most valuable things in life aren't things at all. They are the memories we create with one another.

Lessons from My Journey

I've had my share of triumphs and challenges, and through them all, I've learned:
- Failures are stepping stones. Every setback has shaped me into who I am. Embrace your struggles—they make you stronger.
- Laughter heals. Never take life too seriously. Find joy in the small moments, and don't be afraid to laugh at yourself.
- Love deeply. Love is the most powerful force we have. Give it freely, and you'll never be alone.

Special Memories & My Hopes for You

I remember the summer nights on the porch, telling stories and watching the fireflies. I remember our road trips, the inside jokes, and the moments of quiet understanding. These are the treasures of my life.
As you move forward, I hope you find passion in what you do, kindness in your heart, and strength in times of doubt. Build a life that makes you proud, and never forget where you came from.

Final Words

No matter where life takes you, know that I am always with you. In your laughter, in your kindness, in the traditions we've built together. My love for you is everlasting.

James Carter

With all my heart,
James Carter

 +000 123 456 789
+000 123 456 789

 info@websiteurl.com
name@websiteurl.com

 3222 Blackwell Street
Fairbanks, AK 99701

Crafting Your Message:

➲ **Expressions of Love and Affection:**
Your legacy letter can be a vessel of your unspoken words of love and admiration for your family, creating a lasting memory of your affection.

➲ **Sharing of Core Beliefs:**
Whether religious, spiritual, or just principles, your ethical will can pass on the convictions that guided your life.

➲ **Valuable Life Lessons:**
Our journey is often marked by triumphs and tribulations. Sharing how you navigated life's challenges can be a beacon for your loved ones in their times of need.

➲ **Apologies and Reconciliations:**
If there are unresolved issues or misunderstandings, a legacy letter can be a medium for expressing regret and seeking forgiveness.

➲ **Preserving Family Traditions and Stories:**
This is about keeping the family narrative alive, ensuring that future generations understand their roots and the fabric of their unique history.

➲ **Clarifications on Wealth Distribution:**
Sometimes, the reasoning behind the distribution of your assets can be just as important as the assets themselves. This can provide peace and understanding in the family.

➲ **Imparting Blessings and Hopes:**
Convey your aspirations and blessings for your loved ones, painting a picture of the bright futures you envision for them.

➲ **The Impact and Timing of a Legacy Letter:**
The true power of a legacy letter lies in its ability to touch

hearts and shape perceptions. It's a way to be remembered, to ensure that your values and wisdom are passed down. The decision about when to share this letter is deeply personal. Some may choose to share it during their lifetime, fostering closer family bonds and dialogue, while others might prefer it to be a posthumous message.

- **Preserving and Sharing Your Legacy Letter:**
  Consider keeping your legacy letter with other important estate documents or letting your family know where to find it. It should be easily accessible and shared with those who will cherish it the most.

- **The Journey of Writing Your Legacy Letter:**
  Remember, crafting your ethical will is a journey, not a onetime event. It can evolve as you do, reflecting the growing tapestry of your life experiences. Don't worry about literary perfection; what matters is the authenticity and love that permeate your words.

- **Practical Checklist:**
  To ensure that your legacy letter captures the essence of your life's journey, consider including these key elements:
  - Expressions of love and admiration
  - Core beliefs and values
  - Valuable life lessons and advice
  - Clarifications on wealth distribution
  - Family traditions and blessings

- **A Personal Touch to Your Estate Planning:**
  In our discussions of trusts and estate planning, we've focused extensively on the tangible aspects of legacy. However, as we near the conclusion of this book, it's essential to recognize the power of the intangible. A legacy letter is a testament to the life you've lived and the love

you've shared. It's a cornerstone of your overall estate plan, ensuring that along with your wealth, your wisdom, values, and life lessons are also passed down.

Based on our exploration of legacy letters, we've learned that they lay the emotional foundation necessary to overcome the barriers to comprehensive estate planning. Understanding the importance of this knowledge is just one piece of the puzzle. To truly safeguard our legacy, we must also overcome the myths and barriers that often deter us from engaging in comprehensive estate planning. In the next chapter, we will confront these challenges head on, equipping you with the tools and insights necessary to protect and preserve all aspects of your legacy for generations to come.

Chapter Summary

The Art of Legacy Letters—A Canvas for Life's Wisdom and Treasures Beyond Wealth," emphasizes the importance of legacy letters in estate planning. It explores how these deeply personal documents serve not only as a testament to one's life but also as a vehicle for imparting values, wisdom, and love. Through personal stories and reflections, the chapter highlights the significance of passing down not just material wealth but also the intangible treasures of life's lessons and experiences. It encourages readers to consider crafting their own legacy letters to ensure that their personal ethos and life guidance resonate with future generations, complementing the tangible aspects of their estate plans.

Chapter 10

Overcoming Barriers to Estate Planning

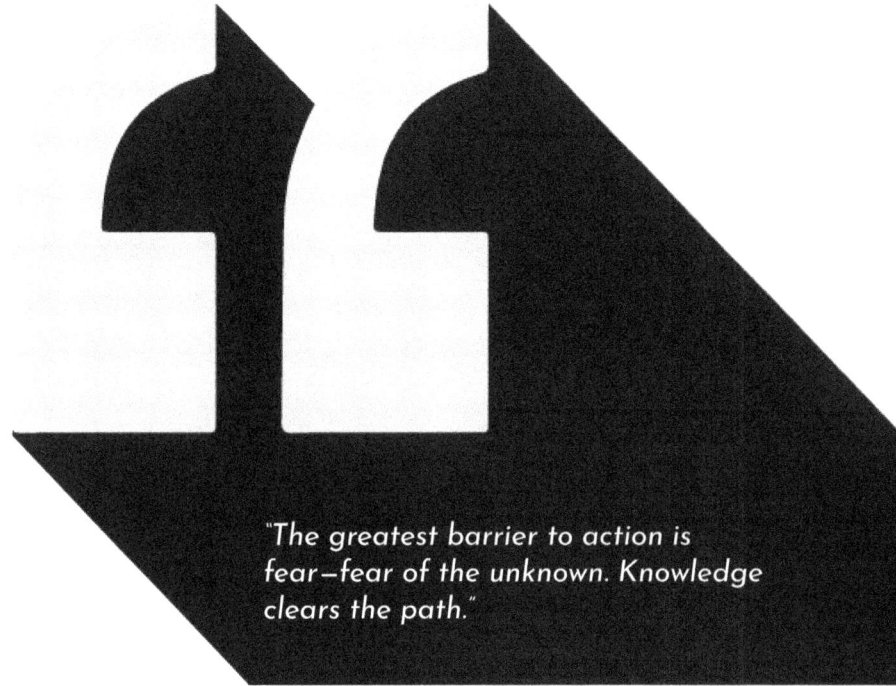

"The greatest barrier to action is fear—fear of the unknown. Knowledge clears the path."

As we conclude this journey, I invite you to reflect on the compelling narrative of the Reels family. Their enduring struggle to maintain their ancestral land on Silver Dollar Road in North Carolina symbolizes the systemic challenges that have stripped countless African American families of their wealth and legacy. Featured in **Forbes**, **The Charlotte Post**, and **ProPublica**, this story serves as a poignant reminder of the dire consequences that can arise from inadequate estate planning and insufficient legal safeguards.

The Reels family's battle extends beyond the mere possession of land; it is a profound testament to dignity, heritage, and the unyielding efforts of generations dedicated to securing a prosperous future. This narrative urges us all to take decisive action, ensuring that the hard-won achievements of our ancestors do not fade away due to myths, misunderstandings, or inaction. Their plight underscores the critical need to dismantle cultural, financial, and emotional barriers that often inhibit families from planning effectively for the future.

Tackling Cultural and Emotional Barriers

In our community, discussing death is often seen as taboo. It's a conversation many avoid, not wanting to confront the inevitable. But avoiding these discussions can have devastating consequences. Estate planning is not about anticipating the worst—it's about preparing for the future. It's an act of love and responsibility, ensuring that our children and grandchildren inherit more than just memories. By shifting our perspective, we can view estate planning as a positive and proactive step towards securing our families' futures.

To tackle these cultural and emotional barriers, it's essential to normalize the conversation around death and estate planning. This can start with community meetings, educational workshops, and open dialogues within families. Sharing stories of both success and caution can help illustrate the importance of planning and encourage others to take similar steps.

Confronting Financial Misconceptions

There's a persistent myth that estate planning is only for the wealthy, that it's a luxury reserved for those with significant assets. This couldn't be further from the truth. Many families have tangible assets that represent both their history and their future. Yet, without proper planning, those assets become vulnerable. Whether you have a modest home or a substantial portfolio, estate planning is essential. It's not just about wealth; it's about ensuring that what you do have is protected and passed on according to your wishes, not left to the whims of state laws or potential family conflicts.

To further dispel these financial misconceptions, it's important to highlight different types of estate planning tools that are accessible to everyone. For instance, a simple will can be created for a relatively low cost and can ensure that your assets are distributed as you wish. Additionally, beneficiary designations on accounts like life insurance and retirement plans can be updated to reflect your intentions, often without any cost.

Overcoming the Barriers of Knowledge and Access

Many people avoid estate planning because they believe it's too complicated or they need extensive legal knowledge to begin. But the key is to start somewhere. Too many families have lost their hard-earned assets due to a lack of knowledge and access to legal resources. This is why consulting with an estate planning attorney is so crucial. They can guide you through the process, explain the necessary steps, and tailor a plan to meet your specific needs. The investment in creating an estate plan is an investment in your family's future.

To make estate planning more accessible, communities can partner with local legal aid organizations to provide free or low-cost estate planning services. Educational programs can also be implemented in schools to teach the basics of financial literacy and estate planning from a young age, ensuring that future generations are better equipped to handle these responsibilities.

Addressing the Present vs. Future Dilemma

It's easy to focus on the immediate needs of today and push future planning to the side. But failing to plan for the future can leave your loved ones in a precarious situation. Estate planning is about balancing today's demands with tomorrow's security. It's about ensuring that the sacrifices you've made and the wealth you've built are not lost due to a lack of preparation.

To address this present vs. future dilemma, setting aside time each year to review and update your estate plan can be a practical solution. This annual review can coincide with tax season or another significant date, making it easier to remember and prioritize. By breaking the process into smaller, manageable steps, estate planning becomes less daunting and more integrated into your routine.

The Myth of Family Harmony

We often assume our families will know what to do when the time comes, that they'll honor our wishes and act in harmony. But the reality is that even the closest families can find themselves in disputes when clear instructions aren't left behind. By providing clear, legally binding instructions for how your assets should be managed and distributed, you can help prevent misunderstandings and conflicts among your loved ones.

To further prevent family disputes, consider having a family meeting to discuss your estate plan. This can help ensure that everyone understands your wishes and the reasons behind them. Additionally, appointing a neutral third party, such as a trusted advisor or attorney, to manage your estate can help prevent conflicts and ensure that your instructions are followed.

Empowering Action Against Inaction

Understanding the barriers that keep us from estate planning is the first step. The next step is taking action. Whether it's creating a simple will or establishing a trust, the key is to start. Any plan is better than no plan, and every step you take towards estate planning is a step towards securing your family's future. Don't let fear or uncertainty hold you back. Inaction can be costly, but proactive planning can make all the difference.

To empower action, consider setting specific, achievable goals for your estate planning journey. For example, you could start by drafting a will within the next month, then move on to setting up a trust within six months. By breaking the process into smaller steps and celebrating each milestone, you can build momentum and ensure that your estate planning efforts are successful.

Practical Checklist:
TAKING THE FIRST STEP

Your Estate Planning Action Plan

To help you get started, here's a step-by-step guide you can use to begin your estate planning journey today:

- **Reflect on Your Legacy:**
  What values, wisdom, and assets do you want to pass on to future generations?

  Write down your intentions for both tangible and intangible wealth.

- **Create or Update Key Documents:**
  Draft a will if you don't have one.

Set up a revocable trust for your major assets, if applicable.

Designate beneficiaries for your life insurance, retirement accounts, and other financial assets.

- **Consult an Estate Planning Professional:**
Schedule a consultation with an estate planning attorney to tailor your plan to your specific needs.

Ask about tools like powers of attorney and healthcare directives to cover all bases.

- **Start Small, But Start Now:**
Choose one manageable task, like listing your assets or gathering important documents, and complete it this week.

Break the process into smaller steps to avoid feeling overwhelmed.

- **Communicate with Your Family:**
Hold a family meeting to discuss your plans, share your wishes, and encourage open dialogue.

Use this opportunity to explain the reasoning behind your decisions to prevent misunderstandings.

- **Review and Revise Regularly:**
Set a reminder to revisit your estate plan annually or after major life events (e.g., marriage, birth of a child, acquiring new assets).

Ensure that it stays aligned with your goals and family's needs.

- **Educate Yourself and Others:**
Attend local workshops or seminars on estate planning.

Share what you've learned with your family and community to reduce the myths and barriers around this process.

Overcoming Obstacles to Make Your Plan

Engaging with legal professionals can feel intimidating, especially if you're unfamiliar with the process. But estate planning attorneys are here to help, to guide you through the complexities, and to work within your budget and time constraints. Remember, the goal is to create a plan that provides peace of mind and security for you and your loved ones. It's about taking control of your future and ensuring that your legacy is protected.

To make the process less intimidating, start by researching local estate planning attorneys and reading reviews from other clients. Many attorneys offer free initial consultations, which can be a great opportunity to ask questions and get a feel for their approach. Additionally, online resources and tools can help you gather the necessary information and prepare for your meeting with an attorney.

Conclusion:
EMBRACING PROACTIVE PLANNING

Estate planning is not just a legal necessity; it's a powerful tool for taking control of your future and safeguarding your legacy. As we've seen, the barriers of myths, cultural norms, and misconceptions can be overcome. By engaging in this vital process, you ensure that your wishes are honored, your assets are protected, and your family's future is secure. This final chapter is not just an end, but a beginning—an invitation to take the lessons learned and apply them to your own life. Remember, estate planning is a fundamental part of responsible adulthood and a crucial aspect of building and protecting generational wealth. Your legacy is yours to shape, and through thoughtful, proactive planning, you can ensure it has a meaningful and lasting impact for generations to come.

In addition to the Reels family's story, numerous other cases highlight the critical need for estate planning in minority communities. Data consistently shows that African American, Hispanic, and other minority families often face significant challenges in preserving their assets due to a lack of estate planning. This often results in the loss of property and wealth, undermining the financial stability of future generations. By addressing these barriers and misconceptions, we can help families secure their assets and build a legacy of generational wealth.

Proactive estate planning is essential for creating and maintaining generational wealth in minority communities. It ensures that assets are protected and transferred according to one's wishes, providing a stable financial foundation for future generations. This not only preserves tangible assets like homes and businesses but also empowers families to support the education and economic advancement of their descendants. By equipping individuals with the knowledge and tools for effective estate planning, we can break the cycle of asset loss and foster a more equitable distribution of wealth.

In conclusion, the story of the Reels family serves as both a cautionary tale and a beacon of inspiration. It underscores that estate planning transcends legal formalities to become a profound moral obligation—an act of love and respect for those who preceded us and those who will inherit our legacy. To truly honor their legacy, we must face and dismantle the barriers that hinder us.

As you turn the final page of this book, I challenge you to take the first step in securing your family's future. Whether it involves drafting a simple will, scheduling a consultation with an estate attorney, or initiating a family conversation about legacy, each action moves you closer to safeguarding your wealth and preserving your story. Remember, estate planning is not about preparing for the end; it's about fortifying the foundation for new beginnings.

Let the lessons from the Reels family, and countless others like them, illuminate your path. Through thoughtful, proactive planning, we can ensure that the sacrifices of our ancestors were not in vain, and that the wealth—both tangible and intangible—they built continues to empower and uplift for generations to come. Your legacy is yours to shape.

Make future generations proud by being the ancestor who broke down the barrier to generational wealth.

Chapter Summary

Overcoming Myths and Barriers in Estate Planning," underscores the importance of confronting and dismantling the obstacles that prevent effective estate planning, particularly within minority communities. It highlights the Reels family's story as a poignant example of the risks posed by insufficient legal preparations, illustrating how cultural, financial, and emotional barriers can undermine the preservation of wealth and legacy. The chapter encourages proactive steps to normalize estate planning discussions, debunk myths that it's only for the wealthy, and enhance accessibility to legal resources. It emphasizes that estate planning is an act of responsibility and love, ensuring that one's wishes are honored and assets are protected for future generations. By educating communities and promoting regular updates to estate plans, this chapter serves as a call to action to secure family legacies and empower future generations with the tools for maintaining generational wealth.

Appendix

Trust Planning Worksheet

This worksheet is designed to help you reflect on and organize the key elements of your trust plan. You can fill it out as a personal record or bring it with you when meeting your estate planning attorney.

01 Successor Trustee Information

Name

Relationship to You

Backup/Alternate Trustee

Notes (why you chose them)

02 List of Assets to Include in Trust

Real Estate (home, land)

Bank Accounts

Investment Accounts

Retirement Accounts
(**note:** usually name trust as beneficiary)

Life Insurance Policies
(note: often name trust as
beneficiary)

Personal Property (jewelry,
art, collectibles)

Business Interests

03 Goals & Intentions for the Trust

➲ Primary purpose of the trust (check all that apply): [ ] Avoid probate [ ] Provide for minor children or dependents [ ] Protect assets from creditors [ ] Ensure smooth family asset transfer [ ] Support charitable causes [ ] Other:

04 Beneficiaries

Name

Relationship

Notes (special instructions, age milestones, etc.)

05 Special Considerations

 Are there beneficiaries with special needs? [ ] Yes [ ] No

 Are there any family conflicts to address?

⊃ Are there any unique assets (family heirlooms, intellectual property)?

03 Notes & Questions for My Attorney

Remember: This worksheet is for your personal preparation and does not replace formal legal advice. Bring it with you when consulting your attorney to help guide a thorough and efficient discussion.

Appendix

Glossary of Key Legal Terms and Concepts

This glossary provides simple explanations of common legal terms related to trusts and estate planning. Use it as a reference as you read and apply the concepts from this book.

1. Trustee

The person or institution responsible for managing the trust's assets according to the trust document and in the best interest of the beneficiaries.

2. Successor Trustee

A backup trustee who takes over management if the original trustee dies, resigns, or becomes unable to serve.

3. Beneficiary

The person or entity (such as a charity) who will benefit from the assets held in the trust.

4. Revocable Trust

A trust that can be changed or revoked by the creator (the grantor) during their lifetime.

5. Irrevocable Trust

A trust that cannot be modified or revoked once it is created, typically offering stronger asset protection and tax benefits.

6. Probate

The legal process of validating a will and distributing assets after someone dies. Trusts help avoid or minimize probate.

7. **Estate Taxes**

   Taxes imposed on the transfer of a deceased person's estate. Proper trust planning can reduce or eliminate estate tax exposure.

8. **HEMS Standard**

   Short for "Health, Education, Maintenance, and Support," this language guides how a trustee can distribute trust funds to beneficiaries.

9. **Spendthrift Clause**

   A provision that protects trust assets from creditors or poor spending habits of the beneficiary.

10. **Funding a Trust**

    The process of transferring ownership of assets (like real estate or accounts) into the name of the trust so it can function properly.

11. **Power of Appointment**

    The right given to a person (often a beneficiary or trustee) to direct how trust assets will be distributed, sometimes even to people not originally named.

12. **Special Needs Trust**

    A type of trust designed to provide for a beneficiary with disabilities without jeopardizing their eligibility for government benefits.

13. Trustee Fiduciary Duty

A legal obligation requiring the trustee to act in the best interests of the beneficiaries, with loyalty, honesty, and care.

14. Living Trust

A trust created during the lifetime of the grantor (person setting up the trust), as opposed to a testamentary trust, which is created by a will after death.

15. Grantor (or Settlor)

The person who creates and funds the trust.

16. Testamentary Trust

A trust created by a will, which only takes effect after the grantor's death and after the will goes through probate.

17. Guardian

A person appointed to care for minor children or dependent adults if the parents or primary caregivers pass away.

18. Durable Power of Attorney

A legal document that allows someone to act on your behalf in financial or legal matters if you become incapacitated.

19. Advance Healthcare Directive (Living Will)

A document that outlines your medical care preferences if you are unable to communicate or make decisions for yourself.

20. Charitable Remainder Trust

A type of irrevocable trust that provides income to beneficiaries for a period, after which the remaining assets go to a designated charity.

21. Generation-Skipping Trust

A trust designed to pass assets directly to grandchildren (or later generations) to avoid double taxation through the children's estates.

22. Pour-Over Will

A type of will that transfers ("pours over") any remaining assets at death into a trust that was set up during the person's lifetime.

23. Grantor Retained Annuity Trust (GRAT)

An irrevocable trust that allows the grantor to pass future asset appreciation to beneficiaries with reduced gift or estate tax.

Index

A
- African American Wealth Disparities ------ 8, 10, 12
- Asset Allocation Strategies ---------------- 28, 29, 30
- Appendix --- 108

B
- Barriers to Estate Planning ---------------- 98, 99, 100
- Beneficiaries ------------------------------- 26, 68, 69, 88
- Business Interests in Trusts ------------------- 26, 28, 29

C
- Charitable Trusts ----------------------------------- 56, 57
- Crafting a Trust ------------------------------- 26, 27, 28

D
- Debt and Wealth ----------------------------------- 10, 12
- Directory of Resources -------------------------------- 110

E
- Estate Planning Conversations ------------- 68, 70, 72
- Estate Tax Planning -------------------------- 48, 56, 58

F
- Funding a Trust -------------------------------- 42, 43, 44

G
- Generational Wealth — 8, 12, 88
- Glossary — 104

I
- Irrevocable Trusts — 26, 30, 31

L
- Legacy Letters — 88, 90

P
- Probate Avoidance — 30, 44, 48

R
- Revocable Trusts — 16, 26, 30, 48

S
- Successor Trustee — 27, 69, 70

T
- Tax Implications — 48, 56, 58, 60
- Testamentary Trusts — 30, 32
- Trust Management — 26, 57, 68

W
- Wealth Preservation Strategies — 12, 88, 90

www.ingramcontent.com/pod-product-compliance
Lightning Source LLC
Chambersburg PA
CBHW050914160426
43194CB00011B/2398